Rhododendrons
& Azaleas

Geoff Bryant

FIREFLY BOOKS

Page 1: Gloriously bright deciduous azaleas.

Page 2: *Rhododendron* 'Yaku Surprise' which has 'Koichiro Wada' as one of its parents.

Page 3: Evergreen azalea 'Betty Ann Voss'

A FIREFLY BOOK

Published by Firefly Books Ltd. 2001

Copyright © 2001 Geoff Bryant & David Bateman Ltd

First Printing

Library of Congress Cataloging in Publication Data is available.

Canadian Cataloguing in Publication Data

Bryant, Geoff
    Rhododendrons & azaleas

Includes index.

ISBN 1-55209-565-7 (bound) ISBN 1-55209-524-X (pbk.)

1. Rhododendrons. 2. Azeleas. I. Title. II. Rhododendrons and azaleas.

SB413.R47B79 2001 635.0'3366 C00-931746-5

Published in the United States in 2001 by Firefly Books (U.S.) Inc.
P.O. Box 1338, Ellicott Station, Buffalo, New York 14205

Published in Canada in 2001 by Firefly Books Ltd.
3680 Victoria Park Avenue, Willowdale, Ontario M2H 3K1

Visit our website at www.fireflybooks.com

Cover design by Shelley Watson, Sublime Design
Book design by Errol McLeary
Typesetting by Jazz Graphics
Printed in Hong Kong by Colorcraft Ltd

Contents

Introduction

Rhododendrons and azaleas are undeniably beautiful, but often when plants are so well known and widely grown, the old adage that familiarity breeds contempt comes into play and eventually their popularity wanes. Rhododendrons and azaleas, however, have never suffered from being so overexposed that they are simply accepted as part of the landscape and largely ignored.

And with those beautiful blooms set so perfectly against that magnificent foliage, when the rhododendrons and azaleas flower even the most jaded gardeners are drawn back to them. But if this book does nothing else, I hope it shows you that rhododendrons and azaleas aren't just about flowers, they are year-round plants with so much more to offer. Look at them closely and you'll see things that you could not have dreamed of.

It is important to note here that the genus *Rhododendron* contains the azalea subgenera (see pages 14-16). Although initially azaleas were considered separate from rhododendrons, it became clear that there was no true division and *Rhododendron*, the genus, covers azaleas also. So when talking in general terms about rhododendrons, I am including azaleas in the discussion.

To the uninitiated many of the rhododendrons can look very similar for much of the year. Of course, they reveal their differences each spring with their unique flowers, but once you get to know them properly you will also find fascination in the details of their foliage and form.

Even if you are not a gardener, rhododendrons are fascinating because of their colorful and interesting history, the way they influenced the exploration and colonization of many parts of Asia and their complex interspecific and environmental relationships. And for the real enthusiast, they are superb subjects for breeding programs because they cross readily, the flower parts are easily accessible and the seed germinates well.

Hardly surprising then, that apart from roses, few genera seriously rival the rhododendron for the position of pre-eminent garden plant. Roses are probably more popular in temperate gardens and many of them flower longer than rhododendrons, but they can't match the foliage and form of the best rhododendrons.

But I don't intend to play favorites. All plants have their merits — rhododendrons far more than most — but unless you understand the basics of their development, cultivation and care the chances are that you will never really be aware of all they have to offer, so read on.

Deciduous and evergreen azaleas make a colorful spring border.

Hardiness Zone Map

This map has been prepared to agree with a system of plant hardiness zones that have been accepted as the international standard and range from 1 to 11. It shows the minimum winter temperatures that can be expected on average in different regions.

In this book, where a zone number has been given, the number corresponds with a zone shown here. That number indicates the coldest areas in which the particular plant is likely to survive through an average winter. Note that these are not necessarily the areas in which it will grow best. Because the zone number refers to the minimum temperatures, a plant given zone 7, for example, will obviously grow perfectly well in zone 8, but not in zone 6. Plants grown in a zone considerably higher than the zone with the minimum winter temperature in which they will survive might well grow but they are likely to behave differently. Note also that some readers may find the numbers a little conservative; we felt it best to err on the side of caution.

°F	Zone	°C
below -50	1	below -45
-50 to -40	2	-45 to -40
-40 to -30	3	-40 to -34
-30 to -20	4	-34 to -29
-20 to -10	5	-29 to -23
-10 to 0	6	-23 to -16
0 to 10	7	-16 to -12
10 to 20	8	-12 to -7
20 to 30	9	-7 to -1
30 to 40	10	-1 to 4
above 40	11	above 4

Hardiness zones are based on the average annual minimum temperature for each zone.

CHAPTER 1

How Rhododendrons Arrived in our Gardens

Rhododendrons have a long and interesting history and I believe that to grow them well you need a feeling for their background. Although there are species and hybrids in all sorts of sizes, shapes and colors, once you appreciate how they are grouped and named and have a feel for their history, everything else falls into place.

Looking around a well-stocked rhododendron nursery can be daunting, but if you understand the significance of phrases such as "it's a yak hybrid", "it's a vireya" or "it's a Belgian indica", you can largely predict how a plant will look and behave.

Rhododendrons were among the earlier flowering plants to develop and the genus has since evolved into over 800 species with many subspecies and natural varieties. Although you certainly don't need to be able to identify each and every one of them, you will enjoy your plants far more if you become familiar with the most influential species that crop up again and again as you look through the parentage of the garden plants.

Most rhododendron species are native to an area bordered by Pakistan in the west, central China in the north, southern India, Vietnam and Burma in the south and Taiwan in the east. This includes the classic Himalayan rhododendron areas of northern India, Tibet, Nepal and southwestern China. Large groups also exist in Japan, Korea, and the rest of temperate Asia, on the east and west coasts of North America, the Caucasus, southern Europe and the tropical regions of Malaysia, Indonesia, New Guinea and northern Australia.

Opposite: *Rhododendron arboreum ssp. arboreum var. kermisinum*

The countryside and general climatic conditions vary enormously throughout this vast range. Specimens can be found growing in all sorts of unlikely places as well as in the moist woodland conditions that we tend to regard as typical rhododendron country. Factors such as altitude, rainfall, temperature and forest cover are all-important influences. So if you are growing species it is a very good idea to thoroughly research the natural habitat of the plant for the vital clues that will help you to provide the ideal growing environment.

Most rhododendron species have been identified within the last 200 years, but the history of rhododendron cultivation goes back much further. Chinese gardens have featured potted specimens for at least 2000 years, though it is unlikely that the Chinese practiced hybridization to any great extent. The evergreen azaleas, in particular those from Japan, probably have the longest history of hybridization: cultivated plants were first mentioned around AD 750. In his book *A Brocade Pillow* (Kinshu Makura), written in 1692 (not long after rhododendron cultivation began in Europe), the Japanese grower Ito Ihei mentions several cultivars that had been grown for many years, a few of which we can still see today. He also describes hybridizing, grafting and other propagation techniques that are remarkably similar to those that we use today.

Most of the species important to hybridizing and developing garden plants were introduced into Europe and North America during the period 1790-1935. Even though nurseries raised new hybrids through much of that period, it was the 20th century that saw the rhododendron explosion. The

This charming sculpture is sheltered by the beautiful *Rhododendron* 'Grand Marquis'.

vast majority of the hybrids in modern gardens have been developed since 1900.

R. *hirsutum* was probably the first species widely cultivated by western European gardeners. Found in the European Alps and introduced into Britain in 1656, it was followed in the mid-18th century by the large and shrubby R. *ponticum*, the deciduous azalea R. *luteum*, and the small R. *ferrugineum*, a close relative of R. *hirsutum*. These were largely local species, however, and for greater variety it was time to look at plants arriving from further afield.

Although we now acknowledge the greater Asian region as the main home of the genus, the first major influx of new plants to arrive in Europe came from among the 28 species native to North America. Many were deciduous azaleas, such as R. *flammeum* (1789), R. *viscosum* (c. 1734) and R. *calendulaceum* (1806), which, when crossed with R. *luteum* (a native of eastern Europe), produced the first hybrid deciduous azaleas. These plants enjoyed some popularity and the range of hybrids increased steadily, though they were scarcely a great sensation.

By 1800 there were still only 12 species in cultivation, but that was soon to change. The eastern European species R. *caucasicum* arrived in Britain in 1803 as a gift to Sir Joseph Banks from Count Pushkin, a Russian horticulturist and father of the writer Aleksandr Pushkin. It was quite widely used in early hybridizing and its influence is still seen today. When crossed with R. *ponticum* it produced 'Cunningham's White', which was a popular cultivar in its own right for many years and is still extensively used as a grafting stock.

The first recorded European rhododendron hybrid is an azaleodendron. That is, a cross between an azalea (a plant of the Pentanthera or Tsutsutsi subgenera) and a rhododendron. *Rhododendron periclymenoides*, an American azalea, was accidentally crossed with R. *ponticum* to produce R. x *hybridum*. The exact date of the cross is not known, but as the

plant was given to the Royal Botanic Garden in Edinburgh, Scotland, in 1814, a date of around 1810 seems most likely. The first deciduous azalea hybrids are dated a little earlier, with confirmed Belgian crosses from 1804.

There are not many true rhododendrons, as opposed to deciduous azaleas, native to North America but those that are generally show extreme hardiness. *Rhododendron catawbiense*, introduced in 1809, was undoubtedly the most important. Its great hardiness (−22°F/−30°C) and large trusses of flowers have had a considerable influence on many of the best hardy garden hybrids. Other American species, such as R. *maximum*, R. *macrophyllum* and R. *minus*, have also been used in hybridizing.

As the 19th century progressed, the emphasis in exploration shifted from the Americas to Asia, particularly the area from northern India through

strikingly marked plants. Third, despite only being hardy to about 10°F (–12°C) it tends not to transfer this tenderness to its progeny when crossed with hardier species, so it introduced the possibility of combining bright colors with hardiness.

The next significant introduction was *R. campanulatum* around 1825. Although not greatly used in hybridization, *R. campanulatum* appears (in conjunction with *R. ponticum*) to have had a considerable influence in the development of mauve and purple cultivars.

The introduction of *R. griffithianum* in 1849 by Sir Joseph Hooker and of *R. fortunei* in 1856 by Robert Fortune (found while searching for new varieties of tea plant) were among the most important of the mid-19th century. The large-growing, fragrant *R. griffithianum*, a native of Sikkim and Bhutan, provided a boldness of foliage and flower that was previously unknown. However, it lacked extreme hardiness and was inclined to be an untidy grower. *R. fortunei* from eastern China is an extremely hardy, fragrant, neat-growing large bush or small tree with magnificent foliage.

Had *R. fortunei* been discovered first it is likely that *R. griffithianum* would not have had the influence that it did. Luckily it wasn't, for it may never have been crossed with *R. griffithianum* and we would not have seen the magnificence of the 'Loderi' rhododendrons that resulted.

Also around this time the first of the tropical vireya rhododendrons were arriving in Europe. These plants, also known as Malesian or Malaysian rhododendrons, have very strikingly shaped and colored flowers but will not tolerate frost, being greenhouse plants in most temperate gardens. Fortunately, greenhouse gardening was all the rage when they were first introduced and vireyas were an instant hit.

Like many of the fashionable greenhouse plants of the 19th century, their popularity waned as hybridizers concentrated on hardy plants for outdoor use and as influential garden authorities emphasized naturalness in gardens. The First World War saw the demise of all but a few of the large European private

southern China to Japan. Venturing into these botanically new areas dramatically increased the range of known rhododendrons. The first Western botanical explorers in the Himalayas found the area to be a vast storehouse of rhododendron species and without doubt the center of the genus. Sir Joseph Hooker's 1850 expedition to Sikkim alone discovered some 45 new species.

The first Himalayan species to arrive in Europe was probably *R. arboreum*. It was discovered in 1799 and arrived in England in 1811. It was an influential plant for several reasons. First, the true species has bright red flowers and was the first large-growing species of this color to be used in hybridizing, bringing new brightness to rhododendron flowers. Second, there are varieties with flowers in shades of pink or white, which introduced an element of chance or genetic instability that has led to some greenhouse collections, but in recent years vireyas have made something of a comeback. Where they can be grown outdoors they are spectacular garden plants.

While rhododendron and deciduous azalea growers concentrated on producing hardy garden hybrids, the direction of evergreen azalea breeding was towards producing florists' plants for forcing into flower. The introduction of the tender *R. simsii* from sub-tropical Asia in 1808 initiated this development. *Rhododendron simsii* tends to produce double flowers, hybridizes freely and can easily be forced into early flowering by giving it greenhouse conditions.

Belgian flower growers were the chief producers of the early *R. simsii* hybrids. This led to the plants being known as Belgian Indica azaleas – indica meaning from the Indies, not a reference to *R. indicum* – a point that has caused confusion ever since. The tenderness of the Belgian Indica azaleas meant that evergreen azaleas were largely ignored as garden plants in Europe. However, when they arrived in the United States in 1838, it was found that they were hardy enough to be cultivated outdoors in many of the southern states and they immediately became very popular.

The hardy, near-evergreen azalea *R. kaempferi* had originally been introduced to Europe as early as 1692 but it was largely ignored. Other hardy species from Korea, Japan and Taiwan, such as *R. yedoense* var. *poukhanense*, *R. kiusianum* and *R. nakaharai*, were much later introductions. They didn't arrive until the late 19th to mid-20th centuries, by which time the center of evergreen azalea breeding had shifted to the United States. This combination of factors, together with their general unsuitability for the less reliable British climate, has led to evergreen azaleas being somewhat undervalued as garden plants in Britain and cool-temperate Europe, though they are very popular elsewhere.

The period 1830-60 saw several vitally important developments for gardeners and botany. The first was improved and faster ships; second, the penetration of mountainous Himalayan and southern Chinese regions; third, the development of the Wardian case; and fourth, the opening up of trade with Japan.

Transporting their finds back to Europe was always a major problem for the early botanical explorers. Even with ever faster and more reliable ships, transporting live plants was a very risky proposition. Most died on the journey, either through extreme variations in the climate or because of poor husbandry on the part of the ships' crews, which was mainly due to a lack of fresh water. The only alternative was to send seed to be germinated and grown on at its destination. However, this added years to the time between collection and the first flowering in cultivation, and was also unsuitable for cultivated specimens that did not reproduce true to type from seed.

The answer was the Wardian case, which was effectively a miniature greenhouse or, as we would probably refer to it today, a terrarium. The Wardian case was invented by a British cleric, Nathaniel Ward, who noticed that small fern sporelings thrived in a closed bottle while all around them the grimy environment of industrial age Britain had killed far tougher plants. This ability of plants to survive and even flourish by recirculating the moisture and gases within an enclosed container was quickly exploited and before long even large specimens were being transported around the world in specially constructed cases.

There remained the problem of getting the plants to the ships, and most collectors still relied on seed as their main source of new plants. Successful seed collection meant being in the right place at the right time and it took hard work to harvest and prepare the seed for shipping. In one of his letters to J.C. Williams, the financier of his 1912-15 expedition, George Forrest mentions processing over 99 lbs (45 kg) of seed, which, considering the small size of rhododendron seeds, is a huge quantity.

It would be difficult to overstate the problems faced by the early botanical collectors. Getting to their destination, collecting and getting out were all fraught with difficulty and danger. And 19th century collectors, whose journeys were usually financed by nurseries, horticultural societies or private benefactors, were expected to be in the field for several years at a stretch – their backers demanded value for money.

Collecting in the rhododendron belt of the Himalayas in the 19th century meant first risking a hazardous sea journey with the possibility of pirates, storms and malnutrition. Then there was the arduous overland trek that could run to several thousand miles there and back, always with the possibility of bandits and disease along the way. And having arrived, there were difficulties with the terrain, the weather, the wildlife and native politics before even starting to collect any plants or considering how to get them out. Several collectors perished on the job and almost all suffered from injuries or diseases.

As we look around our gardens, it is hard to imagine the hardships that were endured to obtain what we now regard as common plants. The cynical would say that it was all done for money, and there is no doubt that a successful new introduction could be worth a large amount, but it doesn't take much research to realize that most of the collectors were genuine enthusiasts not gold-diggers. Which was just as well because they saw very little of the profits made from their endeavors.

Collecting in Japan was thwarted more by political problems than by transportation or climatic difficulties. The rhododendrons of Japan were not nearly as exciting or as extensive as those of the Himalayan region but their potential was probably far more obvious. The heavy-flowering evergreen azaleas and the Japanese species of the Pontica subsection were clearly always going to be excellent garden plants and most were readily available. It was just a matter of being allowed to look for them and to take them home.

These problems were resolved by the actions of Commodore Perry in 1853 and the overthrow of the last Shogun in 1868. Japan was then open to exploration and, along with everyone else, the botanists and collectors were allowed in, and out.

Introductions continued steadily throughout the

Evergreen azalea 'Double Beauty', a Kaempferi hybrid.

rest of the 19th century and into the early 20th century. By 1930 most of the influential species were in cultivation, if not yet greatly used as hybrid parents.

The most significant 20th century introductions include *R. griersonianum* from Yunnan, China, in 1917 and *R. yakushimanum* from Japan in 1932. *R. griersonianum* is a somewhat leggy and tender species with loose trusses of bright orange-red flowers. It was extensively used in hybridizing for many years because its offspring tended to be very heavy flowering; unfortunately they also tended to become untidy growers with easily damaged foliage. Nevertheless many fine hybrids, such as 'Winsome', 'Anna Rose Whitney' and the 'Fabia' grex have *R. griersonianum* in their background.

R. yakushimanum has the kind of compact growth habit and heavy flowering tendencies that make it extremely well-suited to modern small gardens. Discovered as recently as 1920, it caused a minor sensation when first publicly exhibited at the 1948 Chelsea Flower Show. As well as being an almost perfectly formed dome-shaped plant that absolutely smothers itself in flowers, it also has very distinctive foliage. The young growth is covered all over with a soft beige indumentum (felt-like hairs) while the mature leaves are deep green above, slightly rolled at the edges with a thick felt-like white to warm brown indumentum on the undersides. In addition, it is

Rhododendron degronianum ssp. *yakushimanum*

hardy to at least –4°F (–20°C) and will tolerate some exposure to coastal conditions.

Rhododendron yakushimanum quickly became the darling of species fanciers and hybridizers alike. Its influence can be seen in many hybrids and shows no sign of waning. And because it is also popular with species growers, several selected forms are now available.

While we are now unlikely to see any revolutionary new species discovered, it has been a colorful and intricately interwoven history that has brought us to our current state of rhododendron growing. With so many species and hybrids to choose from, hybridizers will always have plenty to work with.

Rhododendron classification

Rhododendrons belong to the Ericaceae or erica family. Other familiar members of this family include the heaths and heathers (*Erica* and *Calluna*), mountain laurel (*Kalmia*), lily-of-the-valley shrub (*Pieris*), cranberry (*Vaccinium*), *Leucothe* and *Andromeda*. Almost all of the ericaceous genera

make good garden plants. Several other genera are often associated with rhododendrons but they do not belong in the same family: *Camellia* is in the Theaceae, *Daphne* in the Thymalaeaceae and *Magnolia* in the Magnoliaceae.

With so many species discovered over several centuries it is perhaps not surprising that the genus *Rhododendron* has been split into more manageable groups and revised several times. Currently the genus is divided into eight subgenera:

Rhododendron
Hymenanthes
Pentanthera
Tsutsutsi
Azaleastrum
Candidastrum
Mumeazalea
Therorhodion

The first four of these subgenera contain by far the bulk of the species – the entire genus but for five species. Of the last four Candidastrum, Mumeazalea and Therorhodion each include only one species (*R. albiflorum*, *R. semibarbatum* and *R. camtshaticum* respectively) while Azaleastrum includes two species (*R. ovatum* and *R. stamineum*).

Subgenera Rhododendron and Hymenanthes include the plants that gardeners recognize as the "true" rhododendrons. Some of these, the lepidote rhododendrons, have small scales on their leaves and make up the subgenera Rhododendron. Elepidote rhododendrons, those without leaf scales, form the subgenera Hymenanthes.

Subgenus Pentanthera covers the deciduous azaleas and Tsutsutsi the evergreen azaleas.

Some of the subgenera are divided into sections, which are further divided into subsections. There are also groupings known as alliances and aggregates composed of very closely related species.

There is no need to fully understand the classification system before attempting to grow rhododendrons, but do try to at least grasp the basic ideas of genus, subgenus, section and species. It will make your understanding of rhododendrons much more complete and is a great aid to identification.

Species names

Biological classification is based on the Linnean system of binomial (two names) nomenclature. Binomial names are also known as proper, scientific or Latin names. Latin (and to a lesser extent Greek) has always been the language of scholars and scientists and is very useful because it is an international language without borders.

The **genus**, the first name, is a grouping of closely related plants that share certain characteristics. The **species**, the second name, is a single plant type within the genus. So there can be many rhododendrons but only one *Rhododendron yakushimanum*.

To qualify as a species a plant must be genetically stable and capable of reproducing true to type from seed. Natural or artificial hybrids, mutants and selected forms are not regarded as new species because they cannot naturally replicate themselves. If they are capable of natural replication yet can still interbreed with the species they may be considered subspecies: naturally occurring, self-perpetuating variations. **Subspecies** (the name is often abbreviated to **ssp** or **subsp**) are usually geographical variations that occur after a population has been isolated for long periods.

The **genera** and species are the last links in a long series of divisions and subdivisions. For most purposes simple identification by genus (*Rhododendron*) and species (*forrestii*) is adequate (remember that azaleas are part of the genus *Rhododendron* too). When written, the whole botanical name should be italicized. The initial letter of the genus name should be capitalized while the initial letter of the species name should be lower case. After the genus that is being referred to has been clearly identified the name is usually shortened to just the initial letter. This book, for example, is about rhododendrons so instead of writing the word out in full it is often abbreviated to *R.*, as in *R. forrestii*.

Variety and cultivar names

Hybrids or unusual forms may occur naturally, and once a plant enters cultivation it is almost certain to be hybridized or developed in some way. Hybrids and cultivated forms fail the first test of a species – they cannot reproduce true to type from seed – so they must be classified in some other way.

Four terms are commonly used to describe these plants: variety (correctly varietas), cultivar, hybrid and clone.

All garden plants are commonly called varieties, but the botanical definition is more precise. A **variety** is a naturally occurring variation of a species, expressed as the abbreviation **var**, as in *Rhododendron forrestii* var *tumescens*. When cultivated it may also be known as a selected form. **Forma** is a term similar to variety but usually differs from the species in less botanically important details.

Cultivar is a contraction of cultivated variety and refers to plants, occurring either naturally or in cultivation, that are not capable of reproducing

Evergreen azalea 'Blaauw's Pink'

naturally and which must be perpetuated by vegetative propagation.

Hybrids are the result of crossing two plants of different botanical classification. That most commonly means two different species within the same genus, though hybrids between genera are also possible – with considerable limitations. When two hybrids are themselves crossed they no longer fully fit the description of a hybrid or a cultivar, so the term culton was instituted. Although a useful term, it is hardly ever used and such plants are usually referred to as cultivars.

Clones are vegetative replicas of the original cultivar or hybrid. As most garden shrubs, unlike say bedding plants, are not reproduced by repeatedly crossing the same parent strains, the term is used somewhat interchangeably with cultivar and hybrid.

A rhododendron like 'Jingle Bells' is a cultivar that was produced by crossing two hybrids. It can be perpetuated by vegetative reproduction only. When written, cultivar names are contained within single quotation marks and are not italicized. Also, in order to avoid confusion with species, such names

should not be in Latin. Until the naming rules were standardized in 1958 there were many cultivars with Latin names; these still stand but new cultivars must have modern language names.

What is an azalea?

Strictly speaking there is no such thing; all azaleas are rhododendrons. Initially the azaleas were classified separately from the rhododendrons but with time it became clear that the division was artificial.

As outlined earlier, the azaleas form two of the eight rhododendron subgenera. The deciduous azaleas make up the subgenera Pentanthera and the evergreen azaleas are classified under Tsutsutsi.

Obviously, deciduous azaleas drop all of their foliage in the fall. But that doesn't mean that evergreen azaleas retain their foliage. While they hold most of their leaves through fall, by the end of winter they can be almost bare, especially in cold climates. Because "evergreen" azaleas can shed

Below: A burst of wild color with evergreen and deciduous azaleas in flower.

By following our cultivar example, 'Jingle Bells', back to its species parents we can learn a lot about its behavior and characteristics. This is especially important when hybridizing because it provides valuable clues about the potential results of crosses.

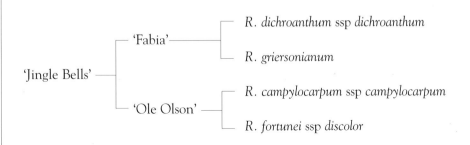

'Jingle Bells'
- 'Fabia'
  - *R. dichroanthum* ssp *dichroanthum*
  - *R. griersonianum*
- 'Ole Olson'
  - *R. campylocarpum* ssp *campylocarpum*
  - *R. fortunei* ssp *discolor*

This parentage provides numerous hints about the nature of the plant. A 'Fabia' background suggests orange flowers (by way of *R. dichroanthum*) and narrow pointed leaves (from *R. griersonianum*). The other parent, 'Ole Olson', may provide the touch of yellow (from *R. campylocarpum*) and may have led to more rounded foliage (through *R. fortunei*). But Halfdan Lem, the hybridizer, also posed interesting questions with this parentage: how would the large round leaves of *R. fortunei* combine with the long narrow leaves of *R. griersonianum*; and how would the dominant apricot-orange color of *R. dichroanthum* be affected by the pink *R. fortunei*?

The end result is a plant that shows little *R. fortunei* influence, but which clearly states its *R. griersonianum* background. 'Jingle Bells' is very much an improved 'Fabia', with brighter colors, bigger flower trusses and healthier foliage. So although the influence of the 'Ole Olsen' parentage is not immediately apparent, a look into the background of 'Jingle Bells' soon reveals where the improvements over 'Fabia' came from.

much of their foliage, botanists prefer the term persistent-leaved to evergreen for these plants.

Evergreen azaleas have two distinct types of foliage, thus they are **dimorphic**. Look closely at the foliage of an evergreen azalea as it develops through the growing season and the two forms will be readily apparent. The new growth that develops in spring is light in texture and quite a bright green. These leaves last through summer but begin to drop in the fall and carry on dropping through winter. The second flush of new growth that develops in summer and early fall is of a heavier texture, is darker green and tends to persist through winter.

A trick sometimes used by growers to make their azaleas more evergreen is to prune off the first flush of growth. This removes the bulk of the leaves that

would have dropped in the fall and also creates a more compact plant.

Special terms

Before we go any further there are two terms that need to be explained as you will see them regularly.

Indumentum

Indumentum, or tomentum, is the felt or hair-like growth that is often found on the underside of rhododendron leaves. Some species, such as *R. yakushimanum*, also show pronounced indumentum on the upper surface of the leaf, though this usually wears off as the foliage matures. Many species exhibit a much-reduced indumentum in the form of a dusty coating on the new growth.

Fragrant flowered *Rhododendron nuttallii*, with its creamy white blooms, is an effective foil for the bright flowers of deciduous azaleas.

The exact function of indumentum is unclear. It may serve as insulation against wind or cold or, as it usually persists on the underside of the leaves where the stomata are located, it may reduce moisture loss through transpiration. Species with young growth that is covered with indumentum are often coastal, so it may protect the tender growth from salt spray. Its function is most likely a combination of all of these things, but whatever the practical value of

Undersides of the leaves of *Rhododendron sinogrande* showing the indumentum typical of this plant.

indumentum it certainly adds to the interest and beauty of many rhododendrons.

Novice growers often worry that the indumentum is some sort of disease. They sometimes even go to the extent of rubbing it off. There would be few commercial growers who couldn't recall at least one customer who had brought in a perfectly healthy indumentum-covered leaf to have its "disease" diagnosed.

Grex

Sometimes, particularly among British hybrids from 1900 to 1960, you may come across the term **grex**, which is Latin and means a flock, herd or troop. It was used to indicate groups of sister seedlings. Among the most famous are the Loderi, Fabia and Naomi grexes. The plants within the groups are identified by the grex name and their own cultivar name, hence we have 'Loderi King George', 'Loderi Sir Joseph Hooker', 'Loderi Venus', 'Fabia', 'Fabia Tangerine', 'Fabia Roman Pottery', 'Naomi Nautilus', 'Naomi Pixie' and 'Naomi Stella Maris' to name a few. Grex is sometimes abbreviated to g., as in 'Naomi' g.

Although group naming is now officially discouraged, the grex was a useful idea. It automatically indicated the relationship between similar plants, which is something that is not immediately apparent when every cultivar has its own completely different name.

CHAPTER 2

Rhododendrons in the Garden

Although massed plantings of rhododendrons can be very impressive, they demand plenty of space and can be somewhat overpowering in a city garden. Because most gardeners choose to use their rhododendrons as part of a wider garden design and because they are compatible with a wide range of plants, you can use rhododendrons in woodland or alpine gardens and rockeries or as part of a well-stocked border or shrubbery.

Woodland

Small to medium-sized rhododendrons (up to 6 ft, 1.8 m high) usually look their best in a woodland setting, where they blend wonderfully with woodland perennials, most of which are suitable for cultivating with rhododendrons. However, it is usually best to avoid perennials with aggressive roots, such as *Acanthus mollis*, or those with rapidly spreading growth. Wood anemones, primroses, hostas and astilbes are indispensable and the range of possibilities is almost unlimited.

Using rhododendrons in a lightly shaded woodland is largely a matter of considering the height and spread of the plants, their moisture and sun exposure requirements, then planting accordingly. Spacing is important because the ground under a rhododendron is heavily shaded and little will grow there. If you plant too closely it will be difficult to establish a good cover of perennials. Conversely, if the rhododendrons are too widely spaced it may be difficult to establish any continuity in the planting. Ultimately, most bushy rhododendrons are about as

Green and white Solomon's Seal (*Polygonatum*) complement the colors of azalea 'Southern Aurora'.

Above: The beautiful flowers of, from left, 'Naomi Hope', 'Sunshine', 'Autumn Tints' and 'Buttercup' are enhanced by the foliage of rhododendrons and cabbage trees (*Cordyline*) as a backdrop. Right: Choosing the right plant for the right space is important. *Rhododendron* 'Martha Isaacson', with its striking dark foliage, makes a shapely focal point in this small garden.

wide as they are high, which is a handy yardstick for deciding on spacing.

If you intend to regularly divide your perennials, don't plant them where such routine disturbance is likely to damage the rhododendron roots. Likewise be careful with woodland bulbs as they will suffer if they have to compete with dense mats of rhododendron roots.

Shrubberies

Many shrubs are suitable companions for rhododendrons. The obvious choices are the other members of the Ericaceae family like *Pieris*, *Kalmia*, *Enkianthus*, *Andromeda* and *Leucothe*, but most plants with a preference for acidic soil are also compatible. Camellias, the larger daphnes and most viburnums do well and are interesting in their own right. Where it can be grown well, *Crinodendron hookerianum* looks marvelous with rhododendrons.

Shrubs with very bold foliage, such as *Fatsia japonica* and the strongly variegated forms of holly (*Ilex*) and *Aucuba japonica*, tend to draw attention to themselves and away from the rhododendron foliage. These brashly foliaged plants are useful for combining with less attractive but functional shrubs. Rhododendrons, however, seldom fall into that category.

Berrying shrubs often make good companions because they provide color at a time when the rhododendrons are usually at their least interesting. Red- or yellow-berried green-leafed hollies blend well, though they can become rather large and may swamp smaller plants. *Skimmia japonica, Sarcococca* species, *Ruscus aculeatus, Stranvaesia davidii* and the smaller cotoneasters crop reliably and don't mind some shade.

Rockeries

Many of the dwarf rhododendrons are natural alpines that are perfectly at home under rockery conditions.

If the rockery is partially shaded so much the better. Alpine rhododendrons generally prefer half a day's sun, while the larger-leafed dwarf hybrids are better with a reasonably bright but mainly shaded location. By varying the plants to suit the exposure you can grow a wide range of species and cultivars.

Because often they are raised, rockeries and alpine gardens tend to be well-drained and on occasions too dry. Incorporate plenty of compost when planting and if there is any possibility of rapid drying, add a few of the water-holding crystals normally used for container plants, just to give the plants a good start.

Shade

Many rhododendrons can be grown in full sun provided the soil conditions are good and they are not exposed to hot dry winds. A little shade is beneficial though. It produces larger, darker leaves

Kurume azaleas 'Christmas Cheer' (in front) and 'Amoena' contrast vividly with spring bulbs and are suitable plants for the back of a rock garden.

and the flowers last longer. In areas with hot dry summers, shade is essential. Small-leafed alpine rhododendrons and most azaleas need to see some sun to keep their growth compact, but you will still need to shade them from the hottest rays to prevent the flowers fading too quickly.

While rhododendrons often cope perfectly well when planted under existing trees, where you have a choice, select your shade trees carefully. Rhododendrons will suffer if the trees are too densely foliaged or their roots are too greedy. Where trees prove to be totally unsuitable they may have to be severely trimmed or removed entirely, which may directly damage the rhododendrons or lead to problems when they suddenly have to tolerate a greater exposure to the sunlight.

Deciduous trees with light foliage cast the best shade. Rhododendrons in the dense shade of conifers and broad-leafed evergreens will become drawn and leggy. However, well-established evergreens that have

Rhododendron pentaphyllum, a deciduous azalea, is a charming and dainty shrub.

been trimmed and thinned are often suitable for underplanting. It is important to avoid trees with masses of densely packed surface roots, such as willows and most birches, as it may be difficult to get the rhododendrons established against such aggressive competition.

Old, high-branched oaks and maples are the ideal shade trees, though magnolias, Japanese maples and dogwoods are more appropriate for small suburban gardens. *Liquidambar*, rowan (*Sorbus* species), *Robinia*, *Gleditsia* and *Styrax* are suitable.

The flowering cherries, plums and almonds (*Prunus*) are also first-rate choices, but sometimes have dense surface roots.

Take your time and choose carefully. It's not just a matter of the trees being attractive; they must be functional too. At a pinch you can scrape by with almost anything provided you are prepared to put in the work. But if you don't have to, why settle for second best?

Unusual growth forms and training

Most rhododendrons and azaleas develop into dome-shaped shrubs or small trees and are left to grow naturally. But some, particularly lanky rhododendrons and the evergreen azaleas, are suitable for training into more strictly controlled growth forms.

Ground covers and cascades

Dwarf rhododendrons often make very good ground covers. Plants such as the bright red 'Scarlet Wonder' and 'Elisabeth Hobbie' are ideal for covering an area while still providing a bit of height, but for truly prostrate ground covers you need to look at evergreen azaleas.

Evergreen azaleas are generally thought of as small, spreading bushes and many of them can be used as ground covers in the same manner as the dwarf rhododendrons, with the added advantage that they will strike roots as they spread. And since the introduction of *R. nakaharai* into hybridizing in the 1960s and '70s, it has been possible to get very low-growing, wide-spreading plants.

The North Tisbury hybrids were the first prostrate hybrid azaleas; they grow to about 4 ft (1.2 m) wide and generally have small red or orange flowers. If planted at the top of a bank or in a large pot they will also cascade.

Espaliers

Tall and spindly rhododendrons, such as 'Fragrantissimum', *R. auritum* and *R. maddenii*, and upright azaleas, such as 'Fielder's White' and 'Orchid Gem' are well suited to espaliering. If pinned to a wall or fence as they grow, with regular tying back and trimming to shape, they will develop a better foliage coverage than they would have as free-standing shrubs. With the flowers concentrated in a single plane, they also appear to flower more heavily.

Standards

Strongly upright evergreen azaleas make good standards. The quickest method of producing a standard is to select a very young plant of an upright variety and train it from scratch. Start with un-branched cuttings and remove the side shoots and lower foliage. Stake the plant as it grows and bush it up by removing the tip when it has reached the desired height, which can be anywhere from 20 to 48 in (0.5-1.2 m).

Hedges

Hedges of evergreen azaleas are very popular in Japan, as are tightly clipped azaleas shaped into boulder-like forms. Making an azalea hedge requires no more than selecting a variety of the appropriate size and spacing, planting and trimming accordingly.

If flowers are important, trim the hedge immediately after flowering and give it a tidy-up just after mid-summer. If a tightly clipped hedge is the aim, trim immediately after flowering and again in early fall. This sacrifices some of the flowers but results in a more evergreen appearance over winter.

Some densely foliaged rhododendrons, most notably R. *ponticum*, can be used for shelter hedges. They will not withstand very heavy trimming but with regular clipping they can be kept reasonably compact.

Container growing

Rhododendrons, and especially evergreen azaleas, are ideally suited to container growing. Worldwide, millions of potted, forced-flowered azaleas are sold each year for indoor use. Because of the shock of forcing and transplanting many do not survive very long, but with the right treatment rhododendrons and azaleas can grow old in containers.

Always use a good quality potting mix, not garden soil. Garden centers often have special rhododendron potting mix that is slightly more acidic than the regular mix. Applications of mild liquid fertilizers and slow-release fertilizer granules should enable the plant to stay in the container for up to two years before re-potting becomes necessary.

When *Rhododendron* 'Bashful' has finished flowering, the hydrangea at its side will take over the limelight, while *Helichrysum petiolare*, trimmed frequently, is interesting in all seasons.

When the time to re-pot arrives, you have a choice: you can either move the plant up to a larger container or undertake some light root pruning and re-pot it in the same container.

Root pruning enables large plants to be kept in their containers, with regular feeding and trimming to keep the foliage lush and healthy. Plants treated this way often flower very heavily. The only limitation is the size of plant that you can handle; removing a large rhododendron from its comparably large pot for its biennial root pruning can be hard work, especially if you have several to do.

Where they need winter protection, vireya rhododendrons are usually grown in containers. Many vireyas are natural epiphytes that are used to perfect soil drainage. Use a very coarse potting mix, such as an orchid or cactus mix blended with a little peat for added moisture retention.

CHAPTER 3

Soil and Nutrition

Understanding the root structure of rhododendrons is the key to growing them well. Look after the roots and the rest of the plant will largely look after itself.

All erica family plants have very fine, hair-like roots that form a densely packed root-ball that is seldom more that 24 in (60 cm) deep, but which is at least as wide as the plant.

Why do rhododendrons have this type of root structure? Many rhododendrons are adapted to growing under deciduous trees where, with an annual dressing of fallen leaves, the soil, over time, becomes composed almost entirely of leaf mold. This type of soil may not be high in nutrients but it is extremely humus-rich and is moisture-retentive yet well-drained. It is not a deep soil (even if it were, the tree roots would remove many of the nutrients from the lower levels), but it is open and easily penetrated by fine roots, water and air. This sort of compost-based soil is usually acidic, and this is why rhododendrons have the preference they do for acidic soils.

Under these conditions rhododendrons have developed highly specialized roots. Most plants have roots with very fine hairs at their tips, which greatly expand the surface area of the root tip and absorb the essential minerals and moisture from the soil. Rhododendron roots do not have root hairs. Instead, the very fine roots perform the functions of root hairs so that the whole surface of the root ball is composed of feeding roots, thus enabling rhododendron roots to make the best use of the small volume of soil they occupy.

Opposite: *Rhododendron* 'Lalique' is obviously content in the soil conditions that have been provided for it.

Rhododendron 'Kimbeth', a shrub growing to about 3 ft (1 m) tall, provides bright color and lush foliage.

There are disadvantages, though. Delicate hair-like roots are the first to suffer in periods of drought or flood, so steady moisture and good drainage are essential. Fine roots suffocate in compacted soils, cannot penetrate heavy soils and cannot move obstacles, such as large stones that may obstruct their progress. All this means that a loose, well-aerated, easily penetrated soil is essential. Avoiding problems comes down to one thing: humus. For rhododendrons, it is virtually impossible to work too much compost or other humus-containing materials into the soil.

Alpine rhododendrons are more adapted to growing in mineral-based soils than in humus-rich leaf mold. However, they tend to occur naturally only in areas with fairly high rainfall and are rarely moisture stressed. The fine roots are an advantage in this

A color-coordinated pair: *Rhododendron* 'Lem's Monarch' and evergreen azalea 'Rosebud'.

environment too, because they enable the plants to make the best use of soils that are frequently leached of nutrients by rain and melting snow.

Many vireyas are epiphytes (they grow on other plants as opposed to in soil). Although they generally only grow in rainforests or in areas that are frequently enveloped in cloud, they are more subject to moisture stress than other rhododendrons and do have somewhat heavier roots as a result. Likewise, deciduous azaleas, which can be found growing in quite dry environments, often have a few woody roots.

Grown under good conditions, rhododendrons are remarkably trouble-free. Apart from direct damage from wind, insects or sunburn, nearly all rhododendron disorders can be traced back to problems with the roots and ultimately the soil, so take the time to get it right.

Preparation

Nothing improves the soil more than natural compost. It is both a fertilizer and a soil conditioner and adds the all-important humus that opens up and aerates the soil while retaining moisture. Visit any natural or artificial woodland area and look at the marvelous loose black soil that forms where the fallen leaves are allowed to build up and decay. That is what your rhododendron soil should look like.

You really can't overdo the compost – add as much as you can and dig it in as deeply as you can. Leaf mold, rotted conifer needles, rotted straw and garden compost are the best materials because they are full of vegetable humus and also provide good levels of nutrients. Stable manure and other animal manures are also good, but they should be mixed with straw and well rotted. Peat, bark chips and rotted sawdust are acceptable but they tend to break down quickly, have little humus and are low in nutrients. Avoid mushroom compost as it is usually quite alkaline.

Making your own compost is the best, and ultimately the cheapest, way of building up your soil's humus content and thereby improving its nutrient levels, aeration, structure, moisture-retention and drainage. No garden should be without a compost pile and no serious gardener should be without compost.

The importance of pH

As moisture is filtered through the soil, the presence of minerals and vegetable matter in the soil will cause variations in its acidity or alkalinity, which are measured on the 14 point pH (potential of Hydrogen) scale.

Based around the neutral point of 7, acidity increases as the pH becomes lower (7-0) and alkalinity increases as it becomes higher (7-14). The scale is logarithmic, so 6 is ten times more acidic than 7, 5 is ten times more acidic than 6 and so on.

Rhododendrons prefer an acidic soil with a pH in the range of 4.5-5.5, but most will grow perfectly

Evergreen azalea 'Red Robin', a Kurume hybrid, is an attractive focal point in front of taller rhododendrons.

satisfactorily with a pH as high as 6.5. Nurseries often sell simple soil test kits that give a reasonably accurate guide to your soil's pH. You can also get a rough indication by using litmus paper. Take a sample of the soil and dissolve it in water, then dip the litmus paper in the liquid. Blue litmus indicates alkalinity and pink to red indicates acidity.

Rhododendrons in the wild sometimes occur on limestone, which is alkaline. However, lime is very soluble and usually travels downward through the soil, so if a humus layer builds up on top of the limestone, the soil may not necessarily be alkaline.

If your soil is alkaline, it may be possible to imitate this type of situation by constructing raised beds for your plants. The lime is unlikely to migrate upward into raised beds, whereas making acidic pockets in limestone soils is only a temporary solution as the lime eventually seeps back.

Nutrients

Rhododendrons have very efficient root systems. Good soil with plenty of compost, combined with regular surface mulching, will usually keep the plants growing well. Establishing the proper nutrient balance not only ensures that your plants will thrive, it also helps them resist climatic extremes, pests and diseases. Regular applications of mild liquid fertilizer and slow-release fertilizer pellets mixed into the mulch will overcome any minor deficiencies.

Plant growth requires that certain elements (nutrients) be present in the soil. Nitrogen (N), phosphorus (P) and potassium (K) are regarded as the "big three". You may have seen the letters NPK on fertilizer packets. They refer to the percentage of these elements in the fertilizer blend. A fertilizer with an NPK of 20-10-15 has 20% nitrogen, 10% phosphorus and 15% potassium by volume.

The pH is also important in determining how efficiently soil nutrients will be used. In general, trace element deficiencies are more apparent in acidic soils but very few soils are so acidic that the effect is greatly noticeable unless the soil is regularly cropped. On the other hand, plants will have difficulty taking up iron and magnesium if the soil becomes too alkaline.

Sources of nutrients

There are two main groups of plant fertilizers, organic and chemical, or to put it another way, natural and artificial. Both forms are available in solid and liquid forms. Solid fertilizers are almost always worked into the soil or used as a soil dressing. Liquid fertilizers are often applied to the soil too, but many are intended to be applied to the foliage. These are known as foliar fertilizers or foliar feeds.

Naturally occurring organic fertilizers, such as animal manures, tend to be relatively mild unless they are very fresh or applied in large quantities. Many add humus as well as nutrients, but some offer

Below: *Rhododendron maddenii* ssp *crassum*

Rhododendron foliage showing the combined effects of nitrogen deficiency and slight frost damage.

only a limited range of nutrients and with repeated use deficiencies may occur. You may need to add chemical fertilizers to ensure a good supply of all the essential nutrients.

Although organic products are better at adding humus, chemical fertilizers are more suited to providing a balanced supply of nutrients and for correcting specific deficiencies.

Chemical fertilizers come as general balanced nutrient blends or as nutrient-specific fertilizers that supply one element or a selected group of elements. All-purpose fertilizers are ideal as a dressing before planting and as a booster in general cultivation, while nutrient-specific fertilizers are primarily intended to correct deficiencies. An example would be the use of iron sulfate or chelated iron to correct iron chlorosis.

Nutrient deficiencies

The most common nutrient deficiencies that occur with rhododendrons are a lack of nitrogen or iron and magnesium chlorosis.

Lack of nitrogen leads to slow growth and an overall yellowing of the foliage that affects the old growth first. Nitrogen is most effectively added by using urea. However, urea is strong; use it at no more than 1 oz per 1½ gallons (25 g per 5 liters) of water or severe burning may result. Milder sources of nitrogen include ammonium sulfate and ammonium nitrate. Make sure these fertilizers are thoroughly watered in.

Chlorotic leaves are usually yellow with distinctly green veins, indicating a lack of iron and/or magnesium. This may be due to deficiencies in these elements (more likely in container-grown plants) or to excess alkalinity preventing the plant from making the best use of the available nutrients.

Because it is often difficult to tell the cause of chlorosis, aim to cover all the possible causes. Mix about 1 oz (20 g) each of iron sulfate and magnesium sulfate (Epsom salts) in 1½ gallons (5 liters) of water. Thoroughly soak the soil around the plants with this mixture. This should correct any deficiencies and the sulfate base of these fertilizers helps to neutralize alkalinity.

Chelated iron is a faster-acting source of iron, but is expensive and requires more care in its application.

Azalea foliage showing the discoloration caused by iron chlorosis.

CHAPTER 4

Assessing your Climate

Which rhododendrons best suit your climate? What is your climate? Obtaining accurate climatic information may be difficult. The local meteorological office can provide accurate data, and almanacs and year-books are a good source of information, but they tend to be very generalized. The weather information in the local newspaper is a good place to start. First, find out the minimum and maximum temperatures recorded in your area, as well as the average number and severity of frosts and the annual and monthly rainfall figures.

Once you have that basic information, study a few books or plant catalogs to eliminate the totally unsuitable plants and to make up a list of possible choices, bearing in mind the other considerations such as ultimate size and flower color. Neighbors are another good source of information about what grows well in your area.

Next, visit garden centers and nurseries to see the plants. It is a great advantage to see the plants in flower before making your final choice. Also, looking at the real thing, rather than a picture in a book, will give you a far better appreciation of the plant as a whole. If you find a plant that appeals, quiz the sales staff or the gardeners about its local performance.

Although this may sound complicated and time-consuming, it is really only applied common sense. The alternative is to buy a few rhododendrons that would appear to be of borderline hardiness for your area and see if they survive.

Rainfall and temperature

Simple annual rainfall figures rarely tell the whole story. Just as important as the amount of rain is the way it is distributed. Rhododendrons prefer moder-

Rhododendrons provide a border for a garden of rock plants and alpines.

ate to high humidity, with regular rain and even soil moisture.

If we look at some of the best areas in the world for temperate-climate rhododendrons we can see that they have somewhat different rainfall patterns, yet still produce similar results.

The Pacific Northwest has a moderate rainfall. Portland, Oregon, averages around 38 in (950 mm) that is evenly spread throughout the year. The rhododendrons grown here are seldom subjected to drought but they may suffer from poor drainage in wet seasons.

The mid-altitude Himalayan home of many rhododendrons includes some of the wettest places in the world and the rainfall is sometimes very seasonal. However, the plants evolved here and can cope with the natural variations. Also, generally excellent drainage and sloping ground means that the plants are rarely waterlogged.

Other areas with high rainfall, such as the southeastern and eastern United States, are also suitable for rhododendrons but good drainage becomes increasingly important as the rainfall level rises.

Rainfall cannot be looked at in isolation; temperature must also be considered. The effect of less rain can be offset by a slightly lower temperature and areas with higher temperatures can cope with more rain. A rainfall of 28 in (750 mm) with an average temperature of 52°F (11°C) has much the same result as 36 in (950 mm) at 54°F (12°C), while 48 in (1200 mm) at 62°F (17°C) is actually a considerably drier climate.

Many alpine and cool-temperate climate rhododendrons prefer climates like those of Portland. In wetter and warmer climates where high humidity is combined with high temperatures, it becomes increasingly difficult to grow alpines, while vireyas and low-altitude Himalayan and Asian species thrive.

Frost

Rhododendrons vary considerably in their degree of frost tolerance. Some are completely intolerant of frost while others can withstand −13°F (−25°C) or lower. Most of the common rhododendron varieties will tolerate 23°F (−5°C) with many capable of withstanding 5°F (−15°C).

Rhododendron 'Snow White', a yakushimanum hybrid. Yaks are more able than most rhododendrons to tolerate occasional salt spray.

Consult your neighbors and go to local nurseries and garden centers to see those best suited to your area. Parks and botanic gardens are also useful. However, unless your local gardens regularly make new plantings or specialize in rhododendrons, their selection may bear little resemblance to that currently stocked by the nurseries, which usually try to keep up with the fashionable varieties.

Choosing hardy rhododendrons does not mean foregoing the fancy cultivars – some of the best are

also the hardiest. Apart from being unable to grow vireyas and some of the more tender fragrant species, such as *R. nuttallii*, gardeners in cold climates are not greatly disadvantaged.

Hardiness is not absolute. Local conditions, seasonal variations, nutrient levels and variations between individual plants all influence the chances of survival. There is also considerable variation even within a species, so although hardiness ratings are useful in eliminating the totally unsuitable plants, they are only a guide.

While the most apparent damage comes from late frosts that destroy the flowers and the soft new growth, repeated freezing and thawing is eventually more serious and may ultimately be fatal. There's not much that you can do to change the minimum temperature apart from providing additional shelter, and late spring frosts are unpredictable, but you can reduce the effects of repeated freezing.

Very hardy rhododendrons tend to have sap that resists freezing, but the liquids in the stems of the more tender plants may freeze if the temperature drops too low. When this happens repeatedly, the bark begins to peel and the stems may split open, much like bursting a sealed bottle by freezing the liquid it contains.

Paradoxically, planting in a site that remains cold and shaded in winter can actually reduce frost damage by lessening the number of times the plant goes through the freezing and thawing process and the rate at which it occurs.

Growing your rhododendrons in woodland conditions not only provides a natural setting but the foliage or branch canopy, however light, also protects the plants from frost damage. Likewise, plants grown against walls and protected by eaves will be considerably less exposed to frost than those out in the open. Shading may cause fewer flower buds to be formed but at least those that form survive to bloom.

Temporary shelters and shadehouses with roll-down plastic covers can provide protection to about 21.2°F (−6°C), but below that you will need to consider treating your tender specimens as green-house plants. Freezing winds can severely desiccate foliage and in very cold areas it may be necessary to wrap plants with burlap as a protection against dry, freezing winds. Bear in mind too that plants grown in containers may freeze solid if left outside, so choose extra-hardy varieties as well as crack-resistant pots. In very cold areas, the plant should be over-wintered indoors.

Wind

Wind can burn flowers and damage tender spring growth. Rhododendrons tend to become more wind-resistant as they mature, but young plants should be sheltered from strong winds, particularly in areas that are prone to hot, dry winds. Fences, hedges, windscreens and temporary shelters all help plants struggling to get established.

Although rhododendrons are seldom thought of as coastal plants, some species, such as *R. yakushimanum*, occur naturally in coastal regions and will tolerate occasional salt spray. Such species tend to have heavy indumentum, particularly on their young growth, which may protect their leaves from the effects of salt spray. It is still a good idea, though, to regularly wash any salt deposits off the foliage.

CHAPTER 5

Choosing Plants

Except when creating a specialist collection, such as the plants of a particular geographic area or hybridizer, choosing rhododendrons is largely a matter of deciding on size, flowers, foliage and flowering season, while always considering your growing conditions. Sometimes other aspects may also be important. For instance, you may want fragrance or a special growth form, but mainly it is size, color and foliage that matter most.

Plant size
While most of the garden hybrids are in the 20 in-8 ft (0.5-2.5 m) range, rhododendrons vary from minute rockery specimens like *R. nakaharai*, which takes many years to reach 6 x 16 in (15 cm high by 40 cm wide), to the tree-like species, such as *R. falconeri*, which can grow to 45 ft (15 m) in the wild.

Deciding on the size of plant is not just a matter of knowing its height and spread; the general growth habit is equally important. Densely foliaged plants often look better than open growers but open plants allow light to penetrate and allow the planting of woodland perennials and small shrubs near them. Consider the overall effect – height, width and foliage cover – when deciding if a plant is suitable.

Flowers

Flowering season
Apart from the vireyas, most rhododendrons have a fairly set flowering season. The exact flowering time of a particular species or cultivar will vary with the latitude and from year to year, but the progression from early- to late-flowering plants through the course of the season is much the same every year.

Rhododendron 'Naomi A.M.'

Temperate-climate rhododendrons develop their flower buds in the fall, overwinter in bud, then flower from late winter to early summer depending on the plant. Flowering is initiated by temperature and day length. This is most evident in the evergreen azaleas: the early-flowering Belgian Indica

Above: *Rhododendron impeditum* 'Blue Steel'
Right: *Rhododendron* 'Carmen' is ideal for rockeries,
growing to only about 2 ft (60 cm) in height.

hybrids will flower as soon as their buds are mature
and often show the odd bloom in the fall, but
Satsuki azaleas are more day-length dependent and
show few blooms until the spring days are over 12
hours long.

If you live in a frost-free climate, early-flowering
azaleas and rhododendrons can be relied upon to add
color from mid-winter. But very early-flowering
rhododendrons are difficult in frosty areas. The
flowers of even the hardiest plants are tender and
few will tolerate lower than 28.4°F (−2°C). Unless
you can protect them, it is best to avoid very early
flowerers.

Most rhododendrons will have finished flowering
by the time of the summer solstice. Indeed, in mild
areas the flowering season will largely be over within
six weeks of the spring equinox.

The later the flowers open, the more likely it
is that their display will be shortened by the increasingly strong spring sun. Some shading, at least from

the hot afternoon sun, is vital if the blooms are to last. Later flowers also have to compete for attention with the roses and early summer-blooming perennials.

By choosing rhododendrons with flowering seasons that correspond with the amount of shelter you can provide from late frosts and early summer sun, it is possible, even in reasonably cold areas, to have a four-month flowering period. In frost-free climates this can be extended to up to eight months because, provided they escape frost, the Indica azaleas will start flowering in the fall and continue on through winter.

Color

There are rhododendrons in almost every shade. All that is lacking is a true blue. There are plenty of mauves and purples that masquerade as blues but there are no gentian-blue rhododendrons.

Certain colors and styles of marking tend to predominate in each of the main divisions. Red, white, mauve and soft yellow are the predominant colors of the true rhododendrons; deciduous azaleas tend towards yellow, orange-red and red; while white and deep pink to magenta-purple are the most common colors among evergreen azaleas.

There are no yellow evergreen azaleas nor are there any deep blackish-purple azaleas, evergreen or deciduous.

Rhododendrons may be single colors or flushed and/or marked with secondary colors. They often have conspicuous contrasting spots in the throat of the flower that seldom develop into a conspicuous flare. Occasionally the flowers are edged with another color.

Hybridizers have not failed to notice these differences and over the years many attempts at crossing between the groups to extend the color range have been made. While we now know that it is genetically impossible to produce yellow-flowered evergreen azaleas by hybridizing with yellow deciduous azaleas, much has been achieved and genetic manipulation offers the prospect of an even greater range of varieties.

Rhododendron 'Mrs G.W. Leak'

Fragrance

'Fragrantissimum' is probably the best known of the scented rhododendrons. Obviously, the name and the age of the cultivar (it was raised before 1868) have a lot to do with it. Unfortunately 'Fragrantissimum' does not really deserve such widespread recognition. It is a straggly, untidy plant that is really only suited to growing as an espalier unless severely trimmed each year, yet it does have a distinctive spicy scent.

It is one of a group of rhododendrons known as edgeworthii hybrids, after *R. edgeworthii*, a species found in northeast Burma, southeast Tibet, northern India and southern China. *Rhododendron edgeworthii* is similar to 'Fragrantissimum' except for a felty indumentum and a slightly stockier growth habit. The flowers are white flushed with pink, as are those of most of its offspring.

Most of the *R. edgeworthii* hybrids were raised between 1860 and 1890 and they tend to be similar to one another. Among the most common are 'Princess Alice', 'Countess of Sefton' and 'Suave'.

There are many other fragrant rhododendrons, mostly species in the Maddenia subsection, such as

R. johnstoneanum, *R. maddenii*, *R. nuttallii*, *R. lindleyii* and *R. dalhousiae*. Lesser known species for the collector include *R. carneum*, *R. coxianum*, *R. decorum*, *R. formosum* var *inaequale* and *R. lyi*.

While the fragrant rhododendrons mentioned so far tend to be rather frost tender, the royal family of fragrant rhododendrons, the Loderii hybrids, are considerably tougher. These magnificent plants will tolerate temperatures down to around –4°F (–20°C). However, they grow to at least 8 ft (2.5 m) high, so allow plenty of room. As with most of the fragrant rhododendrons, white to light pink shades predominate in this group.

The original Loderiis were the work of Sir Edmund Loder and were introduced about the turn of the 20th century. The cross – *R. griffithianum* and *R. fortunei* – has been repeated several times since, most notably by Lionel de Rothschild of Exbury fame, in the 1930s.

Many deciduous azaleas are fragrant, most particularly those with *R. occidentale* parentage, such as

'Delicatissima' and 'Exquisita'. While few evergreen azaleas have any noticeable scent, those with a 'Mucronatum' background, such as 'Alba Magnifica' and 'Fielder's White' are usually lightly scented and can be very effective when they are mass planted. The colors are usually white to mauve.

There are also several fragrant vireya hybrids, most of which have *R. jasminiflorum* somewhere in their parentage. These usually have long, tubular, white to light pink flowers.

Buds

Flower buds might seem an unusual aspect to consider, but often they are attractive and as they are usually clearly visible right through winter they ought to be considered when choosing plants. Buds can be rounded, pointed, tall or squat; they can be smooth, dusty or covered with fine indumentum; and best of all, they carry the promise of spring flowers.

Foliage

Even the most spectacular rhododendron's flowers are only open for a relatively brief time. In terms of year-round appearance, the foliage is far more important than the flowers. Rhododendron foliage is every bit as variable as the flowers and can be just as beautiful too, so take the time to consider the foliage when choosing your plants. Of course, it is hard to ignore the foliage unless you are buying a deciduous azalea out of leaf but it is surprising how often poor foliage is ignored for the sake of a month of pretty flowers.

Size

Most rhododendron leaves are roughly oval in shape with a rounded or slightly pointed tip. Leaf size, however, varies enormously, though it is usually related to plant size, rainfall and temperature. Tiny alpine species, such as *R. intricatum*, have leaves as small as $1/2$ in (10 mm) long, but that is not surprising as they are only very small plants and couldn't support large

Foliage and young growth of Rhododendron arizelum.

leaves. Also, large leaves wouldn't last long in the bitter cold and high winds of the alpine zone.

The largest leaves belong to *R. sinogrande*, native to areas of very high rainfall. Measuring up to 28 in (75 cm) long, these leaves are leathery, glossy, deep green and heavily veined. Its rounded yellow flower trusses are very attractive but they pale into insignificance beside the foliage. Several other members of the Grandia subsection – *R. grande*, *R. macabeanum*, *R. magnificum*, *R praestans* and *R. protistum* – have very similar foliage, but it is seldom more that just over half the size of a mature *R. sinogrande* leaf.

Sun tolerance

It is often said that you can tell the sun tolerance of a rhododendron by the size of its leaves. To a large extent that is true. Small-leafed plants will withstand more sun and often need some exposure, but it doesn't mean that you have to restrict yourself to small-leafed plants in sunny positions.

Sunburn usually appears as a browning in the center of the leaf and is most common in very sheltered sites or if the soil or atmosphere is dry. Keeping the root zone cool and moist is paramount if you want to grow large-leafed rhododendrons in sunny positions, and this will help to raise the atmospheric moisture too.

If you suffer from high summer temperatures combined with low humidity, large-leafed species should be grown in light shade.

Color

Rhododendron leaves come in all shades of green, often with purple, red or bronze tones. Alpines tend to have glaucous (bluish) or purple-tinted leaves while those from mild, wet climates usually have the deepest green foliage.

The best colors are often seen in the new growth, which may be quite different from the mature foliage. This coloring, especially the silver tones, is often caused by a fine indumentum that wears away as the leaf ages. The reddish-brown pigment seen in young leaves is thought to afford tender foliage some

Rhododendron nuttallii showing its distinctive reddish purple new growth.

protection from sunburn. *R. protistum* var *giganteum* and *R. nuttallii* offer striking examples of red new growth.

Fall color

Deciduous azaleas often display brilliant fall foliage color. This starts as a yellowing and progresses through orange to bright red and finally deep blood red. The intensity of the colors is largely dependent on the fall climate: warm days and cold, but not freezing, nights promote the best color.

The spring leaves of evergreen azaleas also color before they drop. Some fall at the yellow stage but others turn red before dropping. The foliage that remains over winter is often intensely colored and

Fall foliage of a deciduous azalea.

can be quite a feature. Azaleas with *R. kaempferi* backgrounds usually show the best winter color.

Indumentum

Indumentum adds to the character of a plant and tends to be a feature that is more prevalent in the species than the hybrids, although *R. yakushimanum* hybrids are often well covered. Species with indumentum that could be considered a feature include: *R. bureavii*, *R. degronianum*, *R. pachysanthum* and *R. yakushimanum*.

Indumentum is often restricted to the undersides of the leaves where it is seldom seen. Such undersurface indumentum is more conspicuous with plants that can be looked up at from below. The Grandia subsection species, such as *R. grande*, *R.*

macabeanum and *R. sinogrande*, all have very large leaves with a conspicuous, silvery buff indumentum.

Scent

Some rhododendrons have aromatic foliage. This may not be noticeable unless the foliage is crushed, but on damp or warm days the scent, often cinnamon-like, can be quite strong. *Rhododendron campylogynum*, *R. cinnabarinum*, *R. glaucophyllum* and *R. hippophaeoides* have noticeably aromatic foliage, as does the hybrid 'P.J.M.' ('P.J. Mezitt').

Bark

A few rhododendrons have attractive reddish brown, peeling bark. It is rarely a feature to rival their flowers or foliage, but it is an extra, adding to the appeal of plants that might otherwise look rather drab in winter. *Rhododendron barbatum*, *R. cinnabarinum*, *R. hodgsonii* and *R. thomsonii* have interesting bark, and *R. arboreum* has distinctive gnarled bark that sometimes peels to reveal a reddish undersurface.

At the nursery

Selecting good specimens is not really difficult because healthy plants usually stand out. They are the ones with the lush, unmarked foliage and the even, well-branched shape. Reject any plants that have discolored, undersized or damaged foliage, are obviously diseased or have uneven growth.

Plants that have been in their containers too long and become pot bound can be difficult to establish because they lack vigorous young roots. Avoid plants with unnaturally small leaves, long spindly branches or roots growing out the drainage holes of their containers.

As far as possible, make sure that the plant matches the description on the label. It is not unknown for plants to be accidentally mislabeled. Because color labels fade, they can be used as a guide but don't rely on them.

CHAPTER 6

The Plants

The plants listed in this book were selected to be representative of garden rhododendrons as a whole. However, because the range of available rhododendrons is so large, varies so much from place to place and new cultivars are always superseding the old, this list can be used only as a guide. Looking at the plants in your local nurseries and assessing them on the basis of your selection criteria is the only practical way to choose.

Hardiness

I have used the United States Department of Agriculture zone system to rate plants according to the zone in which they will survive with minimal protection (see also page 7). The exact point at which frost has seriously damaging effects depends so much on timing, cold duration, plant conditions and other factors that making accurate predictions is very difficult.

If your climate is naturally very variable you may find that you need to make your choice of plants from among those that are hardier than your mini-

Rhododendron rubignosum varies in height between 6-33 ft (2-10 m).

USDA hardiness zones		
°F	Zone	°C
below −50	1	below −45
−50 to −40	2	−45 to −40
−40 to −30	3	−40 to −34
−30 to −20	4	−34 to −29
−20 to −10	5	−29 to −23
−10 to 0	6	−23 to −16
0 to 10	7	−16 to −12
10 to 20	8	−12 to −7
20 to 30	9	−7 to −1
30 to 40	10	−1 to 4

mum temperature might indicate. Once again, look around the gardens in your area and consult specialist growers for the best guide to what applies in your location.

Species

The true enthusiast would say that all rhododendron species are worth cultivating. However, some are rather untidy, rangy growers that have little appeal for gardeners. The following are some of the more attractive, popular or influential species. Many more are available through specialist nurseries and rhododendron societies. The very rare species are often only available as seed. Common subspecies, varieties and cultivars are included with the species. All are evergreen unless otherwise stated.

R. arboreum

Tree Rhododendron This tree, found from northern India to southern China, usually grows to around 39 ft (13 m) tall in cultivation with a narrow, cylindrical crown. It has leathery, deep bronze-green, 8 in (20 cm) long leaves with whitish or rust-colored undersides. The flowers, bell-shaped in globular heads of 15-20 opening in early spring, are usually red, though forms with white or deep pink flowers are common. This species was an early intro-duction and is a parent of many cultivars. Zone 7.

R. arizelum (syn R. rex subsp arizelum)

A large-leafed species native to northern parts of Burma, India and Yunnan, China. Despite having leaves up to 14 in (35 cm) long with heavy indumentum, it is a Falconeri not a Grande series rhododendron. Its flowers are variable and may be cream or various shades of yellow or pink, usually with a red blotch. They are carried in trusses of up to 25 blooms and open in early spring. Zone 7.

R. augustinii

First described in 1886, this species from southern China and Tibet has bronze-green leaves that darken in winter. While it is usually seen as a 5 ft (1.5 m) shrub, it can develop into a 29 ft (9 m) tall tree and from mid-spring it is smothered in loose clusters of two to six, small, funnel-shaped, blue or violet blooms. Zone 6.

R. aurigeranum

Native to Papua New Guinea and found in forest clearings, rocky areas or grassy slopes at moderate altitudes, this vireya grows to 8 ft (2.4 m) tall with orange to orange-yellow, funnel-shaped flowers. It is popular with hybridizers. Zone 10.

R. auritum

This Chinese and southeast Tibetan species is rare in the wild, where it is found on sheltered low-alpine cliffs. It is an open upright shrub 36 in-10 ft (90 cm-3 m) tall, and has small leaves with rusty brown scaling on the undersides. The small, tubular, bell-shaped flowers open from early spring and are pale yellow or cream. Zone 8.

R. bureavii

This beautiful, 10-16 ft (3-5 m) tall, Chinese shrub is renowned for its foliage, especially the dense underside indumentum. The flowers are white flushed red, often with deep pink markings. *Rhododendron bureavii* can be tricky to grow, demanding perfect drainage and shade from the hot summer sun. Zone 6.

R. burmanicum

Famous as the parent of many of the first yellow-flowered hybrids, this 3-6 ft (1-2 m) high shrub is found in southwest Burma at 8640-9600 ft (2700-3000 m). It is a rather frost-tender plant with aro-matic, scaly, bronze-green leaves and slightly scented yellow flowers in clusters of up to six blooms. Zone 9.

R. calendulaceum

Flame Azalea A deciduous azalea, found from West Virginia to Georgia, that develops into a spreading bush around 11 ft (3.5 m) tall and wide. The flower color varies with the season, location and climate but is usually orange to red and rarely yellow. The blooms are funnel-shaped, open in late spring and are carried in trusses of five to seven blooms. Many orange-flowered azalea hybrids have this species in their background. Zone 5.

R. callimorphum

Callimorphum means "with a lovely shape", which is an apt description. It is a very neat, 24 in-6 ft

(60 cm-1.8 m) tall shrub from Yunnan, China, and northeast Burma with attractive, glossy, deep green, medium-sized leaves. The bell-shaped flowers, in trusses of five to eight blooms, are white to rose-pink, sometimes with purple flecks and open from mid-spring. Zone 7.

R. catawbiense

Mountain Rosebay Native to the eastern United States, *R. catawbiense* was one of the most influential species in the development of hardy hybrids. It really does have everything: relatively compact growth (around 10 ft / 3 m tall), dense, shiny, deep green foliage and showy cup-shaped flowers in trusses of up to 20 blooms. The flowers open from late spring and are pink, rosy pink, lilac-purple or white. **'Album'** is a heat-resistant form with white flowers that open from pink buds. Zone 4.

R. ciliicalyx

This western Chinese shrub grows quickly to form a 5-10 ft (1.5-3 m) mound of narrow long leaves with brown scaled undersides. Its flowers, which are sometimes lightly scented, are funnel- to bell-shaped, white- or pink-tinted, around 3 in (8 cm) long and in clusters of three. They open from early spring. Zone 7.

R. cinnabarinum

Native to the Himalayan region and northern Burma, this aromatic upright shrub grows to as much as 20 ft (6 m) in height. It is very distinctive, having peeling red-brown bark and narrowly oval, deep green to blue-green leaves. The flowers are pendulous and tubular, around 2 in (5 cm) long and open from mid-spring. Usually orange, the trusses of three to five flowers may be red, salmon-pink, pink, yellow, apricot or combinations of colors. Zone 6.

R. concinnum

This tree-like species from Sichuan, China, has dark blue-green, elliptical leaves and 2 in (45 mm) long, funnel-shaped flowers in small clusters. The flower

Above: *Rhododendron ciliicalyx*
Below: *Rhododendron concinnum* var *pseudoyanthinum*

color is wide-ranging, including white and all shades of lavender and purple to wine-red, often with contrasting throat markings. **R.c var *pseudoyanthinum*** is a compact shrubby form with flowers in shades of purple-red. Zone 7.

R. dauricum

Found naturally in some very cold winter areas of China, Mongolia, eastern Russia and northern Japan, this semi-deciduous 24 in-5 ft (60 cm-1.5 m) tall shrub is often in bloom shortly after mid-winter. It has red-purple, purple, pink or white, $^{1}/_{2}$-1 in (12-25 mm) long, funnel-shaped flowers and scaly, deep green, $1^{1}/_{2}$ in (35 mm) leaves that develop bronze tones in winter. Zone 5.

R. davidsonianum

An upright open shrub growing to around 6 ft (2 m) tall, this western Chinese species has lance-shaped leaves that are deep green on top with scaly undersides. The 2 in (5 cm) long funnel-shaped blooms in trusses of two to six are of variable color, usually white or white suffused with pink but often pink or lavender and sometimes green- or red-flecked. Zone 7.

R. edgeworthii (syn R. bullatum)

Popular in the mid-19th century for hybridizing, this fragrant-flowered Himalayan species unfortunately lacks hardiness and is inclined to be rather rangy. It grows to around 5 ft (1.5 m) tall and has bronze-green, lance-shaped leaves with thick fawn-colored indumentum. The flowers, in groups of two or three, are 3 in (8 cm) long, funnel-shaped, white flushed with pink and open from mid-spring. Zone 9.

R. elliotii

Found at moderate altitudes in northern India and usually seen as a 6 ft (2 m) tall shrub, *R. elliotii* is renowned for its flower color, which is an intense red with very dark spotting and white-tipped anthers. The flowers, in trusses of around 10 blooms, are 2 in (5 cm) long bells that open from mid-spring. Zone 9.

R. ferrugineum

Alpine Rose Native to the Pyrenees and the Alps, and in cultivation as early as 1739, this small shrub has small, deep green leaves with scaly brown undersides. Its bell-shaped flowers are less than 1 in (25 mm) long and open from mid-spring. Carried in trusses of six to eight blooms, they are usually deep pink but may be any shade of pink. Zone 4.

R. forrestii

Popular with hybridizers for creating dwarf heavy-flowering bushes, and found at up to 14,700 ft (4600 m) in Yunnan, Tibet and Burma, this dwarf, spreading shrub seldom exceeds 6 in (15 cm) high. It has rounded, deep green leaves and bright red, waxy, $1^{1}/_{2}$ in (35 mm) long, bell-shaped flowers carried singly or in pairs, opening from early spring. Zone 8.

R. fortunei

Influential in the development of garden hybrids, this Chinese species is a shrub or small tree with mid-green, oval leaves up to 8 in (20 cm) long. Its flowers are around 3 in (8 cm) wide. They open pink, fade to white and are fragrant. The large, rounded trusses open from mid-spring. **R.f. subsp *discolor*** has flowers with a yellow-green blotch and **R.f. subsp *fortunei*** has pale pink to lavender flowers and leaves with purple-red petioles. Zone 6.

R. genestieranum

This unusual Himalayan species, with foliage perhaps more reminiscent of *Kalmia* than *Rhododendron*, is usually seen as a 4 ft (1.2 m) high shrub. The flowers, in heads of up to 12 blooms that open in early spring, are very distinctive, being deep red with a dusty blue-gray bloom and protruding anthers. Zone 9.

R. glaucophyllum

A dwarf shrub found from eastern Nepal to Burma at up to 11,500 ft (3600 m), this species has small, bell-shaped flowers in loose clusters of up to 10 blooms. The flowers are deep pink, fading to white at the petal tips and have conspicuous calyxes. Zone 8.

Rhododendron genestieranum

R. glischrum

This open, often rather leggy shrub from Yunnan, China, and nearby parts of Burma and Tibet benefits from being shaped when young. Kept compact, it is an attractive bush with rounded trusses of white or pale pink flowers with reddish blotching. Zone 8.

R. griersonianum

Influential in many early to mid-20th century hybrids, this 5-10 ft (1.5-3 m) tall, open shrub from western China and northern Burma has light green, lance-shaped leaves that, along with the petioles and young stems, are bristly. The flowers, in trusses

of up to 12 blooms, are funnel-shaped and an unusual shade of pinkish orange-red, sometimes with darker flecks. Zone 8.

R. griffithianum

Another influential hybridizing species, this shrub or tree from the Himalayan region has peeling red-brown bark and bright green, oblong leaves up to 12 in (30 cm) long and large. White to rose pink flowers are occasionally spotted green and are carried in trusses of four to five blooms. They are scented and have conspicuous calyxes. Zone 8.

R. hyperythrum

This heat-tolerant Taiwanese shrub grows to 5 ft (1.5 m) tall with dense, compact growth and narrow, deep green leaves with rolled edges. Its funnel-shaped flowers open from pink buds and are white with occasional red-purple flecks. They are around 2 in (5 cm) long in trusses of 10 or more. Zone 8.

R. impeditum

Usually very dense and compact in cultivation, this western Chinese alpine species has tiny, aromatic, silvery blue-gray leaves and is smothered in small, funnel-shaped, lavender to purple flowers carried singly or in pairs from early spring. Zone 4.

R. jasminiflorum

A vireya native to the Malay Peninsula, this 8 ft (2.5 m) tall shrub has bright green leaves in whorls of three to five. Throughout the year it produces trusses of between five and eight scented, tubular, white flowers up to 2 in (5 cm) long. Zone 10.

R. javanicum

This epiphytic or terrestrial vireya, native to Malaysia and Indonesia, usually grows to around 5 ft (1.5 m) tall in cultivation. It has oval leaves up to 8 in (20 cm) long and slightly fragrant, large-lobed, funnel-shaped flowers in loose trusses. The flowers are around 1½ in (35 mm) long and wide in orange to orange-pink or red shades with cream or yellow centers. Zone 10.

Rhododendron keleticum

R. johnstoneanum

From northern India and sometimes epiphytic in the wild, this large shrub has bristly, elliptical leaves up to 3 in (8 cm) long. Its flowers are scented, 3 in (8 cm) long, creamy white or pale yellow funnels, sometimes with red or yellow spots, and open from early spring. **'Double Diamond'** has pale yellow, double flowers with darker spots. Zone 7.

R. kaempferi

Torch Azalea This Japanese evergreen azalea is very hardy, a feature capitalized on by hybridists, though it loses much of its foliage in extreme cold. The leaves are hairy, elliptical and 1½ in (35 mm) long. Funnel-shaped flowers open from mid-spring and are red to orange-pink, occasionally white, sometimes with purple or red flecks. Zone 5.

R. keiskei

Variable, but usually around 24 in (60 cm) high, this Japanese shrub has lance-shaped leaves that are bronze-green when young. The flowers are 1½ in (30 mm) wide, pale to bright yellow, widely flared funnels that open from early spring. **'Yaku Fairy'** is a densely foliaged, near-prostrate form with reddish new growth and bright yellow flowers. Zone 5.

R. keleticum (syn R. calostratum subsp deleticum)

A tiny evergreen shrub seldom over 12 in (30 cm) high. It has relatively large, wide open, near-flat flowers that are usually purple and occurs in Yunnan, China, and nearby parts of Tibet and Burma at up to 14,400 ft (4500 m) in altitude. A superb rockery or bonsai plant. Zone 6.

R. kiusianum

Kyushu Azalea From Kyushu, Japan, this dense, mounding, evergreen azalea is usually less than 3 ft (90 cm) tall, with tiny, hairy, purple-green leaves that darken in winter. From mid-spring the foliage is hidden by small purple, pink or white flowers. An important parent of the Kurume azaleas, there are many cultivated forms including **'Benichidori'**, salmon-pink flowers; **'Hinode'**, bright red flowers; **'Komo-kulshan'**, white or pale pink flowers with darker petal tips; and **'Mt. Fuji'**, white flowers. Zone 6.

R. lacteum

A Himalayan species with beautiful pale yellow flowers often tinted with pink. The foliage is also impressive: dark green with fawn-colored indumentum and up to 8 in (20 cm) long. Growing to around 5 ft (1.5 m) tall, grafted plants often develop a better shape than those on their own roots. Zone 7.

R. leucaspis

This western Chinese and Tibetan shrub grows to around 3 ft (90 cm) tall with small, bristly, blue-green leaves. The flowers open very wide – almost flat – and are white, often slightly pink-tinted with brown anthers. They are up to 2 in (5 cm) wide, in clusters of three blooms. Zone 7.

R. lindleyi

A tall shrub from northern India, Nepal and Bhutan, it is often epiphytic in the wild. The leaves are large and it bears trusses of four to six fragrant, white, funnel-shaped flowers up to 4 in (10 cm) long. It is advisable to trim the plant when young to develop a neat shape. Zone 9.

R. lochae

This vireya found in northeast Queensland, Australia, grows to around 6 ft (1.8 m) tall and has 3 in (8 cm) long oval leaves. The flowers are tubular with large lobes, deep red and 1½ in (35 mm) long. They are carried in trusses of two to seven blooms. Zone 10.

R. luteum

Pontiac Azalea Found from eastern Europe to the Caucasus, this deciduous azalea is around 6 ft (2 m) tall and has bristly, lance-shaped leaves. Its narrow, funnel-shaped flowers are bright yellow and sweetly scented, around 1½ in (35 mm) long, in trusses of up to 12 blooms. Zone 5.

Rhododendron lacteum

Below: *Rhododendron lindleyi*

Rhododendron lochae

R. lyi

Although inclined to be an open bush with rather sparse foliage, fragrant flowers are the appealing feature of this 3-5 ft (1-1.5 m) high Chinese shrub. They are white to cream with a yellow blotch and are occasionally flushed with pink and appear over a long season in clusters of four. Zone 9.

R. macabeanum

Capable of growing to 48 ft (15 m) tall, this species from northern India is large in all its parts. The leaves are very dark green, heavily veined, leathery and up to 18 in (45 cm) long with white indumentum on the undersides. In early spring rounded trusses of up to 20 pale yellow, bell-shaped flowers open. They are 2-3 in (5-8 cm) long and blotched with purple. Zone 8.

R. maddenii

This often epiphytic species, found from the Himalayan region to Vietnam, is an open, sometimes leggy shrub with 6 in (15 cm) long, scaly, bronze-green leaves. Its flowers are tubular to funnel-shaped, up to 4 in (10 cm) long and scented. They are usually white with a yellow basal blotch but are sometimes tinted pink. Zone 9.

R. maximum

Great Laurel, Rosebay Rhododendron Developing into a large shrub or small tree, this hardy eastern North American species has slightly hairy, 6 in (15 cm) long, elliptical leaves and blooms late. Its flower trusses carry 15-20 white to deep pink, bell-shaped flowers with greenish spotting. Its great hardiness has been used to advantage by hybridizers. **'Red Max'** has a neat growth habit and dark flowers; **'Mt. Mitchell'** has leaves with red streaks and marbling. Zone 3.

R. molle

This deciduous azalea is found in temperate East Asia, grows to 6 ft (1.8 m) tall and was important in the development of the Mollis hybrids. It bears large, densely packed trusses of sometimes fragrant, 2 in (6 cm) long, funnel-shaped yellow or orange flowers from mid-spring. **R.m. subsp *japonicum*** from Japan is an upright shrub with bright red, orange-red, pink or yellow flowers and brightly colored fall foliage. Zone 7.

R. montroseanum

One of the Grande series rhododendrons with very large leaves, this small tree from southeastern Tibet

Rhododendron mucronulatum

bears trusses of up to 20 deep pink, bell-shaped flowers. The leaves are 8-12 in (20-30 cm) long with heavy veining and a silvery indumentum on the undersides. Zone 8.

R. mucronulatum

One of the few deciduous rhododendrons that is not an azalea, this hardy 5 ft (1.5 m) tall shrub from northeast Asia and Japan has scaly, lance-shaped

Below: *Rhododendron montroseanum*

leaves and produces small, pink to purple, funnel-shaped flowers from late winter. In mild areas it will flower in mid-winter. **'Cornell Pink'** has very early, soft, pure pink flowers and yellow-orange autumn foliage; **R.m. var *taguetti*** is a very early-flowering near-prostrate variety from Korea. Zone 4.

R. nakaharai

This evergreen azalea from Taiwan is nearly prostrate, a feature that has endeared it to hybridists. It has tiny, pointed, elliptical leaves that are very hairy. Its flowers are small, orange-red funnels that open in early summer. It is an excellent rockery, bonsai or ground cover plant. **'Mariko'** has pinkish red flowers and **'Mt. Seven Star'** is a densely foliaged form with relatively large, deep orange-red flowers. Zone 5.

R. nuttallii

Native to the Himalayan region and a marvelous plant in all respects, this tall shrub or small tree has large, deep green, slightly glossy leaves that are strongly red-tinted when young. Mid- to late spring sees the opening of its trusses of between three and seven powerfully fragrant, bell-shaped, creamy white to pale yellow flowers. Zone 9.

Rhododendron occidentale 'Delicatissima', a deciduous azalea.

R. occidentale

Western Azalea This 6-8 ft (1.8-2.4 m) tall, deciduous azalea from the western United States has slightly hairy, elliptical leaves and very fragrant, 3 in (8 cm) wide flowers that are funnel-shaped and carried in trusses of up to 12 blooms. The flower color is usually white or pale pink with a strong yellow flare, but may be red, yellow or orange-pink and occasionally the flare is maroon. The foliage turns red and copper shades in the fall. Zone 6.

R. oreodoxa

A large shrub or small tree, this Chinese species has an open, upright growth habit and leaves with blue-green undersides. Its flowers, in trusses of 10 to 12 blooms, open very early and are usually pale pink, sometimes with purple spotting. **R.o. var *fargesii*** (syn R. *erubescens*) is a deep pink-flowered form. Zone 6.

R. pachypodum

Found in western Yunnan, China, this is one of the Maddenii rhododendrons. Unlike its relatives, its white to pale yellow flowers have little fragrance.

They are quite large and appear early in spring in clusters of two to five flowers. The leaves are a bright green with rusty scales on the reverse and the bush grows to around 6 ft (1.8 m) tall. Zone 8.

R. pachysanthum

Cultivated as much for the indumentum on its foliage as its flowers, this small, densely foliaged Taiwanese native has bell-shaped, white to pink flowers in trusses of up to 20 blooms. The upper sides of the young leaves are coated in a dense brown indumentum that eventually wears off, though the fawn-colored indumentum on the lower surfaces remains. Zone 8.

R. parryae

Similar to the better known *R. dalhousiae*, though usually a neater plant, this 5-10 ft (1.5-3 m) high shrub from Assam, India, is notable for its pale bark and mildly scented, white flowers. It has large, bright green leaves and the flowers, which often have a yellow-orange blotch, open in mid-spring. Zone 9.

R. pentaphyllum

Five-leaf azalea This deciduous azalea from central and southern Japan grows 6-13 ft (2-4 m) tall and has leaves that are arranged in distinctive whorls of five at the branch tips. The leaves are fairly small and rounded and the flowers are light pinkish red wide-open bells. Zone 7.

R. ponticum

Found in Europe and the Middle East through to southwest Russia, this vigorous large shrub or small tree has glossy, deep green, oblong to lance-shaped leaves and 2 in (5 cm) long, funnel-shaped flowers in trusses of 10 to 15 blooms that open in late spring. Their color is usually purple but can be lavender, pink, white flushed with pink or, rarely, maroon, often with yellow, ocher or brown flecks. Invasive in some areas. **'Cheiranthifolium'** has light purple flowers and long, narrow, wavy-edged leaves; **'Variegatum'** has dark cream-edged leaves with cream stripes or flecks. Zone 6.

Rhododendron prunifolium, the plumleaf azalea.

R. prunifolium

Plumleaf azalea This deciduous azalea from the southeast United States flowers late, usually after the summer solstice, and prefers more shade than most deciduous azaleas. It is around 5-6 ft (1.5-1.8 m) high with narrow, oval leaves and trusses of four or five funnel-shaped flowers. Color range is orange-red to red, occasionally orange or yellow. Zone 6.

R. pseudochrysanthum

A 3-5 ft (1-1.5 m) high shrub native to Taiwan, this species develops into a neat, rounded bush with dense foliage and heavily flowered trusses of white to pale pink flowers that open from deep pink buds. The interior of the flowers is often red-spotted. There are several cultivars with varying bud colors and foliage. Zone 8.

Rhododendron rupicola

R. rubignosum

This 6 ft (2 m) tall shrub from the Himalayan region is inclined toward open rangy growth and should be trimmed when young to keep it compact. It has 3 in (8 cm) long, lance-shaped leaves that are tinted purple-bronze when young. The flowers, carried profusely in trusses of up to 10 blooms, are usually lavender, pink or white with spotting. Zone 7.

R. rupicola

This alpine species from the mountains of Burma and western China is a wiry-stemmed 2 ft (60 cm) shrub with tiny leaves and clusters of small, funnel-shaped, light purple flowers in early spring. Like most alpines, it prefers a cool climate. Zone 5.

Rhododendron scabrifolium var *spiciferum*

R. russatum

A 45 in-4 ft (45 cm-1.2 m) tall shrub from western China, this alpine species has small, scaly, deep green, elliptical leaves. Funnel-shaped flowers are about 1 in (25 mm) wide in trusses of four to 10 blooms. The flower color is variable, usually a shade of pink or purple or sometimes white. The growth habit also varies with compact and upright forms. Zone 5.

R. scabrifolium

This is a western Chinese shrub, often a rather untidy bush but which makes up for it with masses of tiny flowers. If trained when young it can be kept to around 3 ft (1 m) tall. The flowers, in clusters of two or three blooms, are small funnels in white or various shades of pink. **R.s. var *spiciferum*** (syn *R. spiciferum*) from southern and central Yunnan, China, has very small leaves on wiry stems and tiny flowers with long stamens. Zone 8.

Rhododendron scopulorum

R. scopulorum

A slightly frost-tender, fragrant-flowered, 6 ft (2 m) high shrub found in eastern Tibet, this species is notable for its pleasantly scented cream flowers that open from biscuit-colored buds. Its leaves are deep green and densely clothe the bush. Zone 9.

R. sinogrande

Found in high rainfall parts of the Himalayan region and famed for its huge leaves, in early spring this tree-sized rhododendron produces rounded trusses of 20 or more, 3 in (8 cm) long, cream to pale yellow, bell-shaped flowers with a basal crimson blotch. The leaves are the largest in the genus: up to 3 ft (90 cm) long, though usually considerably smaller. They are deep green and heavily veined with a buff or fawn indumentum. Zone 8.

R. sperabile

This 3-5 ft (1-1.5 m) high evergreen shrub is found in northeast Burma and Yunnan, China, at around 9600-11,200 ft (3000-3500 m) in altitude. Its leaves are about 4 in (10 cm) long with a covering of fine hairs. The bell-shaped, crimson-red flowers are often damaged by bumblebees, which split them to gain access to the nectar. Zone 8.

Rhododendron sinogrande has the largest leaves of any rhododendron.

R. thomsonii

Found in the Himalayas and western China, this variable species is usually seen as a small tree around 13 ft (4 m) tall. It has oval leaves and peeling red-brown bark. Its trusses of between 10 and 12 flowers open from early spring and are usually blood-red but also occur in shades of pink with crimson spotting. When mature *R. thomsonii* is very heavy-flowering. Zone 6.

R. viscosum (syn R. serrulatum)

Sweet Azalea, Swamp Azalea, Swamp Honeysuckle
Found in damp depressions and along riverbanks in eastern North America, this 5-15 ft (1.5-4.5 m) tall deciduous azalea has lance-shaped leaves that are deep green on top, blue-green below. The narrow, funnel-shaped flowers are cream tinted with pink and have a spicy fragrance. Opening after the leaves, they are $1^{1}/_{2}$ in (35 mm) long, in clusters of 12 or so blooms. This species includes those formerly classified as *R. coryi*, *R. serrulatum* and *R. oblongifolium*. Zone 3.

R. williamsianum

This dense-foliaged shrub from Sichuan, China, is notable for its rounded to heart-shaped foliage. The leaves are a fairly light green, which contrasts with the bronze new growth. The bush grows to as much as 5 ft (1.5 m) tall and in mid-spring bears loose clusters of two or three bell-shaped, 2 in (5 cm) long, mid-pink to rose flowers, sometimes with darker flecks. Zone 7.

R. yakushimanum (syn R. degronianum subsp yakushimanum)

Native to Yakushima Island, Japan, this dense, mounding, 1-3 ft (30-90 cm) tall shrub is renowned for its neat growth habit and the heavy fawn-colored indumentum on the undersides of its leaves. The flowers are white or pale pink opening from deep pink buds in mid-spring and are carried in rounded trusses of up to 10 blooms. There are many cultivars including: **'Exbury Form'**, a perfect dome of deep green with light pink flowers; **'Ken Janeck'**, a strong grower with large leaves and pink flowers; **'Koichiro Wada'** a dome-shaped bush with white flowers opening from deep pink buds; and **'Yaku Angel'**, a vigorous bush with large trusses of white flowers. Some authorities consider R. yakushimanum to be a subspecies of R. degronianum, but the usual preference is to list it separately. Zone 5.

R. yedoense var poukhanense

Korean Azalea This is a tough azalea from Korea. Nominally evergreen, it loses much of its foliage in very cold conditions. It is up to 5 ft (1.5 m) tall and has sparsely hairy, lance-shaped leaves and slightly fragrant, 2 cm (5 cm) wide, funnel-shaped, deep pink to lilac flowers. It has been used extensively in hybridizing to add hardiness. Zone 5.

R. zoelleri

This vireya from Indonesia, Papua New Guinea, and the Moluccas can reach 20 ft (6 m) tall, though it is usually far smaller. Its trumpet-shaped flowers are a particularly bright shade of yellow and orange with orange-red lobes. Zone 10.

Rhododendron williamsianum

Rhododendron cultivars

Rhododendron cultivars, unlike azaleas, are generally not divided into groups – being most often simply referred to by their cultivar name. And while there may be recognizable styles, – alpine, grande, yak, etc. – except by the cognoscenti they are usually differentiated simply by size. This is not a very reliable method because rhododendrons are long-lived and continue to grow throughout their lives. Very old specimens can be extremely large. Consequently, I haven't tried to be precise about size. As a rough guide, dwarf is under 18 in (45 cm) when mature, small is less than 4 ft (1.2 m), medium is 4-8 ft (1.2-

2.4 m) and anything that matures at over 8 ft (2.4 m) tall is large.

'Alice' An *R. griffithianum* hybrid dating from 1910 and still popular. It has 6 in (15 cm) long leaves and with age becomes a large bush. Its upright trusses of bright pink blooms with lighter centers appear mid-season. Zone 6.

'Alpine Meadow' This small bush is reminiscent of 'Snow Lady' and other *R. leucaspis* hybrids. It has rounded, mid-green leaves covered in fine hairs and from early spring it is smothered in clusters of creamy white flowers. Zone 7.

'Anah Kruschke' A late-flowering, medium-sized *R. ponticum* hybrid with deep green leaves and funnel-shaped, red-purple blooms in trusses of seven and 12. Zone 5.

'Anna' A medium-sized shrub with narrow, deep green leaves. Large trusses, each with seven to 12 red buds, open in mid-spring. The flowers are funnel-shaped and deep pink fading to pale pink with red throat markings. Zone 7.

'Anna-Rose Whitney' This large shrub has 6-8 in (15-20 cm) long, mid-green, oval leaves and deep pink, trumpet-shaped flowers up to 4 in (10 cm) wide. They open late and are carried in trusses of up to 12 blooms. Zone 6.

'April Glow' A densely foliaged, medium-sized, mounding bush with rounded leaves and reddish new growth that reveal its *R. williamsianum* heritage. Masses of deep pink flowers open from mid-spring. Zone 6.

'Arctic Tern' Raised by Caperci of the U.S.A. but popularized by Cox of Glendoick, Scotland, this small, wiry-stemmed shrub has narrow leaves and produces clusters of tiny white flowers in mid-spring. Perhaps more reminiscent of a daphne than a rhododendron and best out of the hot sun. Zone 7.

Above: *Rhododendron* 'April Glow'
Opposite: *Rhododendron* 'Arctic Tern'

'Babylon' A medium-sized, dense, mounding bush with narrow, deep green leaves up to 6 in (15 cm) long and luscious conical trusses of up to 15 funnel-shaped, white to pale pink flowers with brown throat markings. It flowers early. Zone 6.

'Bibiani' This medium-sized *R. arboreum* hybrid was raised in 1934 by the famous English breeder Lionel de Rothschild. It has large, dark green, heavy textured leaves and deep red, 2 in (5 cm) wide, bell-shaped flowers in trusses of 11-15 blooms in early spring. Zone 7.

'Billy Budd' This small shrub has elliptical leaves with a slight indumentum. It blooms mid-season with flat-topped trusses of 10 to 12 waxy, bright red flowers. Zone 6.

'Black Sport' Bred by American Ben Nelson and introduced in 1982, this hybrid is of uncertain

parentage but probably has *R. ponticum* origins. It has pointed, deep green leaves and unusual deep reddish purple flowers with a very dark blotch. Zone 6.

'Blue Diamond' This small *R. augustinii* hybrid has bronze-green leaves and in early spring is smothered with clusters of small flowers that are lavender to mid-blue in color. Regular pinching back keeps it compact. Zone 6.

'Blue Peter' Probably an *R. ponticum* hybrid, this medium-sized bush was introduced in 1933 by the English company of Waterer, Sons & Crisp. It has glossy deep green leaves and frilled mid-spring trusses of lavender-blue flowers with a prominent purple flare. Zone 6.

'Brickdust' This small plant forms a dense mound of 2 in (5 cm) long, rounded leaves with masses of loose clusters of bell-shaped flowers that are typical of an *R. williamsianum* hybrid. The blooms are dusky orange and appear mid-spring. Zone 6.

'Broughtonii Aureum' (syn 'Norbitonense Broughtonianum') An azaleodendron with the rather complex parentage of (*R. maximum* x *R. ponticum*) x *R. molle* this is an unusual, if rather weak, semi-deciduous plant with narrow, drooping leaves. Its flowers are a soft pinkish yellow with a cinnamon blotch and open quite late. Zone 6.

'Bruce Brechtbill' A sport of 'Unique', this medium-sized shrub has pink flushed with yellow flowers. The deep green oblong leaves are lush and its conical trusses open early to mid-season. Zone 7.

'Carmen' This neat, small, evergreen shrub has waxy, textured, deep red, bell-shaped flowers that show its *R. forrestii* background. Raised in 1935 by Rothschild of England, it is a superb plant for large rockeries. Zone 7.

'Carousel' Around 32 in (80 cm) high when mature, this hybrid dates from 1965 and is a compact alpine-

style plant with trusses of small soft pink flowers with darker markings. Zone 5.

'Cheer' This medium-sized American hybrid by Shammarello was introduced in 1958 and, as befits a plant with 'Cunningham's White' in its parentage, it is very easy to grow, tough and adaptable. Flowers in various shades of pink smother the bush from early spring. Zone 5.

'Cherry Custard' A small Canadian hybrid that shows its 'Fabia' heritage in its flat trusses of 10 to 12 blooms that open yellow from orange-red buds. It is a low, spreading plant with narrow, pointed, elliptical leaves. Zone 7.

'Christmas Cheer' Always one of the first to bloom, this old medium-sized *R. caucasicum* hybrid has light to mid-green elliptical leaves and trusses of five to 11 funnel-shaped, white and pale pink flowers opening from deep pink buds. The bush is hardy in Zone 5 but frosts will destroy the flowers.

'College Pink' This medium to large hybrid from New Zealand has lush foliage and large, rounded trusses of deep pink flowers in mid-spring. It is a tough, easily grown bush that is attractive at any time of year. Zone 7.

'Cornubia' A large, vigorous, *R. arboreum* hybrid with slightly puckered mid-green leaves up to 6 in (15 cm) long. It blooms very early with a marvelous display of trusses of bright red funnel-shaped flowers. The plant is hardy in Zone 8 but the flowers are damaged by late frosts.

'Corry Koster' This hybrid of uncertain parentage raised by the Dutch breeders M. Koster & Sons dates from around 1909. Very popular in its time and occasionally used as a grafting stock, it has fairly large leaves and an abundance of deep pink flowers. Zone 6.

Rhododendron 'Cherry Custard'

'Countess of Haddington' Many fragrant rhododendrons are untidy bushes but this 1862 hybrid is a neat medium-sized bush with slightly glossy, bronze-green foliage. Its large, bell-shaped flowers are white flushed with pink, pleasantly scented and carried in heads of three to five blooms. Zone 9.

'Cream Crest' Masses of creamy yellow flowers smother this small bush in mid-spring. For the rest of the year it is a mound of bronze-green foliage that needs some sun to develop its best color. A good choice for large rockeries. Zone 7.

Rhododendron 'Corry Koster'

'Creamy Chiffon' One of the few double-flowered rhododendrons, 'Creamy Chiffon' is a compact medium-sized shrub with rounded leaves and bronze new growth. Its flowers are a soft creamy yellow opening fairly late from orange, pink-tinted buds. Some shade and perfect drainage are essential. Zone 7.

'Crossbill' This 1933 *R. spinuliferum* x *R. lutescens* hybrid has clusters of unusual creamy yellow and orange-red flowers with protruding stamens. While being an easily recognized plant it probably wouldn't have remained popular except that it flowers very early and remains compact with light pinching back. Zone 7.

'Cunningham's White' Although perhaps better known as a grafting stock, this medium-sized shrub dating from 1850 is still attractive. It is very tough and adaptable with mid-green oval leaves and late, frilled trusses of white flowers with a yellow-green blotch. Zone 5.

'Cupcake' An American-raised, dwarf, *R. yakushimanum* hybrid and one of the first of its type to bloom in spring, 'Cupcake' is a neat mound of foliage with deep pink flowers that have a hint of orange. Zone 6.

'Dainty Lass' This New Zealand-raised, small to medium-sized shrub has lush mid-green foliage and compact heads of white flowers opening from pink buds. Zone 7.

'Dora Amateis' One of the few *R. minus* hybrids, this small shrub has aromatic, pointed, elliptical, deep green leaves that are bronze when young. In early spring the foliage disappears under masses of clusters of three to six, white, funnel-shaped flowers. Good drainage is vital. Zone 5.

'El Camino' A large shrub with equally impressive foliage and flowers. The leaves are not large but the

Rhododendron 'Cupcake'

foliage is luxuriant. The flowers are wide-open pink funnels with a lighter center and darker spotting in trusses of around 12 blooms. Zone 6.

'Elisabeth Hobbie' A small *R. forrestii* hybrid with rounded, 2 in (5 cm) long, deep green leaves and red-tinted petioles and new growth. Its flowers are bell-shaped, bright to deep red, in clusters of five to seven blooms, opening mid-season. Zone 6.

'Elizabeth' Typical of the British *R. griersonianum* hybrids of the 1930s, 'Elizabeth' is a medium-sized, rather open bush with narrow, pointed leaves and bright red, funnel-shaped flowers in lax trusses of six to eight blooms from mid-season. **'Elizabeth Red Foliage'** has red-tinted young growth. Zone 7.

'Else Frye' From mid-spring this medium-sized bush has very fragrant, yellow-centered, white flowers with a light flushing of pink. The foliage has a heavy texture. Zone 8.

'Fabia' grex This collection of cultivars, resulting from a 1934 *R. dichroanthum* x *R. griersonianum* cross by the Welsh breeder Aberconway, had enormous influence on the development of modern hardy hybrids in yellow and orange shades. They are small to medium-sized shrubs with pointed, elliptical

leaves and trusses of three to seven bell-shaped blooms in soft orange and pink tones. **'Roman Pottery'** has unusual terracotta-colored flowers; **'Tangerine'** has bright orange-pink flowers. Zone 7.

'Fastuosum Flore Pleno' Raised before 1846 and still one of the few double-flowered rhododendrons, the trusses of up to 15 flowers on this large shrub open mid- to late spring. They are deep lavender with greenish yellow throat markings. Zone 5.

'Fireman Jeff' This American hybrid, introduced in 1977, has intensely red flowers backed by large calyces of the same color creating a hose-in-hose effect. It is a small bush with dark foliage. Zone 7.

'Fragrantissimum' This medium-sized, rather open, *R. edgeworthii* hybrid remains popular because of the scent of its large, funnel-shaped, pink-flushed white flowers. They are carried in loose trusses of three to seven blooms, opening mid-spring. The foliage is bronze-green, tapering to a sharp point. Zone 9.

'Frank Baum' This medium-sized American hybrid is named after the author of *The Wizard of Oz*. It is a late bloomer and has blooms in trusses of 10 to 14

Rhododendron 'Fragrantissimum'

flowers that open late and heavy dark green leaves with red-tinted petioles. Zone 6.

'Freeman R. Stephens' This shrub is large in all its parts. It can reach 6 ft (2 m) tall and 10 ft (3 m) wide, has leaves up to 6 in (15 cm) long with large, bright pinkish red, mildly scented flowers in upright trusses of 10 to 15 blooms. Zone 6.

'George's Delight' Typical of the style of plant popular since the late 1960s, this distinctively colored small shrub has lush mid-green leaves, dense growth and spectacular rounded trusses of soft yellow and cream flowers with pink margins. Zone 7.

'Gills Crimson' Bred in the early 1900s, this *R. griffithianum* hybrid is a large shrub with glowing, translucent red flowers in rounded trusses atop lush foliage. It demands space but is well worth finding a place for. Zone 7.

'Ginny Gee' This dwarf *R. keiskei* hybrid is a superb plant for a rockery, with small, deep green leaves and tiny, white suffused with pink, funnel-shaped flowers that smother the bush from early spring. Zone 7.

'Goblin Orange' One of the Goblin grex of 'Break of Day' x *R. griersonianum* hybrids raised by Rothschild in the late 1930s, 'Goblin Orange' is a small bush that bears orange-red flowers with lighter markings, backed by large calyces. The foliage is light green with scaly undersides. Zone 7.

'Golden Wit' This small shrub has a spreading growth habit and rounded bright green leaves. Its bell-shaped flowers, which open mid-season, are soft golden yellow with red or red-brown markings and are carried in loose clusters of up to nine blooms. Zone 7.

'Grace Seabrook' A medium-sized shrub, 'Grace Seabrook' has lush, deep green foliage with a light indumentum. Its tight, rounded trusses of large, bright red, funnel-shaped flowers open in early spring. Zone 6.

'Halfdan Lem' Bred by and named after the famed hybridizer, 'Halfdan Lem' is a medium-sized shrub with large, dark green leaves on reddish petioles and stems. Bright red, funnel-shaped flowers in trusses of up to 13 blooms open mid-season. Zone 6.

'Hansel' Grown as much for the rusty indumentum on its new growth as for its subtly shaded pink and salmon flowers, this small shrub has neat, compact growth and flowers in mid-spring. Zone 6.

'Harvest Moon' A medium-sized fairly early-flowering shrub raised by Kosters' Nursery of Holland. It has large, rather glossy leaves and showy trusses of creamy yellow flowers with red markings. Zone 6.

'Hello Dolly' This 'Fabia' hybrid is a densely foliaged, medium-sized bush with mid-green leaves that have a buff indumentum. Light orange flowers borne in loose clusters open in mid-spring from

Rhododendron 'Honeymoon'

orange-red buds. They have large calyxes that create a semi-double effect. Zone 6.

'Honeymoon' A beautiful hybrid, 'Honeymoon' shows considerable *R. wardii* influence and is medium-sized, forming a dense mound of lush, deep green foliage. The flowers, borne in flat trusses of up to 15 blooms opening from mid-season, are soft yellow with a hint of orange. Zone 7.

'Hotei' This is a medium-sized hybrid, one of the first really hardy, relatively small, yellow-flowered rhododendrons. It has rounded, bright green leaves and bright yellow, bell-shaped flowers, borne in rounded trusses of up to 12 blooms from mid-season. Zone 7.

'Hydon Hunter' With dense foliage, this small to medium-sized shrub has dark green, 4 in (10 cm) long leaves and mauve fading to pale pink flowers in trusses of up to 14 blooms from late mid-season. Zone 7.

'**Imperitrin Eugenie**' An early-flowering medium-sized shrub, this hybrid has pale pink flowers with darker stamens and brownish spotting. Not the most spectacular flower but it blooms heavily and is reliably tough. Zone 6.

'**Irene Bain**' A small *R. yakushimanum* hybrid raised by Dr. J.S. Yeates of New Zealand who was better known for his deciduous azaleas than his "true" rhododendrons. It is a neat plant with frilly cream flowers edged in pink. Zone 7.

'**Janet Blair**' This is a large shrub raised by Leach of the United States in the early 1960s and has influenced many hybrids. It is a strong grower with deeply veined leaves and pale yellow-pink flowers with a yellow-green flare and a pink flush. Zone 5.

'**Jingle Bells**' A 'Fabia' hybrid, this one forms a neat, small bush with a dense covering of narrow, deep green leaves. Orange, bell-shaped flowers in lax trusses of between five and nine blooms open from orange-red buds and fade to yellow, smothering the plant from mid-spring. Zone 7.

'**Kaponga**' Reminiscent of 'Cornubia', but later and heavier blooming at a younger age, this New Zealand-raised *R. arboreum* hybrid has narrow foliage and tightly packed, rounded trusses of deep red flowers. Zone 8.

'**Kilimanjaro**' Medium to large, this 1940s Rothschild hybrid has marvelous deep green foliage and huge, red, funnel-shaped flowers in conical trusses of up to 18 blooms. It flowers from mid- to late season and is always impressive. Zone 7.

'**Kimbeth**' A small, heavy-flowering, rounded shrub that quite literally smothers itself in rosy pink flowers from mid-spring. An ideal plant for the front of a border or a large rockery. Zone 6.

'**Lalique**' Bearing deep green foliage, this is a medium to large hybrid with generous trusses of pale pink fading to white flowers opening from bright pink buds. It blooms in mid-spring. Zone 7.

'**Lem's Aurora**' This is a compact, small to medium-sized bush with dark green leaves and rounded trusses of crimson flowers that have light golden yellow centers and calyxes. It blooms in mid-spring. Zone 6.

'**Lem's Cameo**' Undoubtedly one of the most beautiful hybrids in flower and foliage, 'Lem's Cameo' has also been very influential in the development of later plants. It forms a medium-sized mound of deep green, glossy leaves with rich, bronze new growth. The funnel-shaped flowers open in mid-spring, borne in trusses of up to 20 blooms, and are delicate shades of apricot-pink and creamy yellow. Zone 7.

'**Lem's Stormcloud**' An upright, medium to large plant with mid-green, elliptical leaves. Its flowers, carried in trusses of up to 15 blooms, are deep wine red with a white to pale pink throat and long stamens. They open from late mid-spring. Zone 5.

'**Little Ben**' This small shrub has a dense, many-branched growth habit that can be made even more compact by tip pinching. Its flowers, opening mid-spring in pairs or small clusters, are bright red backed by conspicuous calyxes. Zone 8.

'**Loderi**' grex This group of *R. griffithianum* x *R. fortunei* seedlings dates from around 1900. They are very similar to one another and have large mid-green to slightly glaucous leaves and upright trusses of white to mid-pink, funnel-shaped, fragrant flowers. They are large, tree-like plants that are very impressive in full bloom. '**Horsham**', white flowers with a faint pink blush; '**King George**', pink buds opening white; '**Pink Diamond**', soft pink flowers; '**Sir Edmond**', large pale pink flowers; and '**Sir Joseph Hooker**', light to mid-pink flowers. Zone 6.

Opposite: *Rhododendron* Loderi 'Horsham'

'Mariloo' A hybrid (and also part of a grex), 'Mariloo' has heavily textured, rounded leaves with an unusual blue-green to bronze bloom. The flowers are a very pale milky yellow, bell-shaped and carried in large trusses. They open mid-season from yellow-green buds. It is hardy in Zone 8 but the new growth is very tender.

'Markeeta's Prize' This vigorous medium-sized to large shrub with impressive leathery foliage has huge bright red flowers that are held above the foliage, making them stand out even more clearly. Zone 6.

'Maurice Skipworth' Rather tender and medium-sized, this New Zealand-raised hybrid appeals mainly for its delicately shaded, fragrant blooms. It is not a neat plant unless pinched back but that is forgiven in early spring as the pink buds open to reveal luscious cream flushed with pink flowers. Zone 9.

Rhododendron 'Mount Everest' has slightly perfumed flowers.

'Moonstone' A small to medium-sized *R. williamsianum* hybrid with rounded mid-green leaves. From early spring it is smothered in clusters of greenish white to pale cream, slightly pendulous, bell-shaped flowers. Zone 6.

'Moonwax' This is a medium-sized shrub with narrow, oval leaves and waxy cream flowers with pale mauve tints. The flowers are mildly scented and carried in large trusses of up to 12 blooms that open in mid-spring. Zone 7.

'Mount Everest' A large bush, 'Mount Everest' has narrow, mid-green leaves and slightly fragrant flowers that are bell- to funnel-shaped and white with red-brown spotting. They are massed in trusses of between seven and 11 blooms and open early. Zone 6.

'Mrs G.W. Leak' Instantly recognizable in bloom, this medium to large bush has upright trusses of nine to 12, light pink, funnel-shaped flowers with a beautiful red flare, blooming from mid-spring. They stand out from a great distance. The leaves are light green and very sticky, especially when young. Zone 6.

'**Mrs Mary Ashley**' This medium-sized British hybrid is very heavily foliaged and compact with rounded, fairly light green leaves. From mid-spring it is covered in bright pink flowers with lighter centers. Zone 7.

'**Nancy Evans**' With 'Hotei' x 'Lem's Cameo' parentage, this small to medium-sized shrub had to be something special. It is worth growing for its foliage alone – rounded, deep bronze-green leaves with reddish new growth. The bell-shaped flowers are striking too, being deep golden yellow opening from orange buds in trusses of 15-20 blooms with large calyxes creating a hose-in-hose effect. Zone 7.

'**Naomi**' This Rothschild grex includes some beautiful plants. The best known Award of Merit form is a large, densely foliaged shrub with mid-green to slightly glaucous leaves and waxy flowers in light biscuit and pink shades, carried in large trusses that open in mid-spring. '**Nautilus**' has superb foliage and orange-flushed pink flowers with a green throat; '**Pink Beauty**' has deep pink flowers. Zone 6.

'**Olin O. Dobbs**' Famed for its heavy, waxy flowers of intense red-purple, this medium-sized American hybrid has lustrous, deep green leaves up to 6 in (15 cm) long. The flowers are funnel-shaped and carried in conical trusses of 11-15 blooms that open from mid-spring. Zone 5.

Rhododendron 'One Thousand Butterflies', worth growing for its name alone.

'**One Thousand Butterflies**' This is a medium-sized 'Lem's Cameo' hybrid with deep green leaves and large mid-spring trusses of funnel-shaped flowers. Their appeal lies in their coloration: a butterfly wing pattern of deep pink with a pale pink center and dense red spots radiating from the center. Zone 6.

'**Paprika Spiced**' A small to medium-sized 'Hotei' hybrid, so-named for the color of its funnel-shaped flowers, which are cream and orange with reddish brown spotting overlaid with gold tones. The flowers are carried in trusses of up to 15 blooms and are backed by large calyxes that are also spotted. Zone 6.

Rhododendron 'Olin O. Dobbs'

'Patty Bee' This pretty dwarf hybrid develops into a mound of small, bright green, elliptical leaves. From mid-spring it is smothered in six-flowered clusters of soft yellow, funnel-shaped blooms. Ideal for rockeries or containers. Zone 6.

'Percy Wiseman' This *R. yakushimanum* x 'Fabia Tangerine' hybrid is a small to medium-sized bush that combines the best characteristics of its parents. Densely clothed in narrow, deep green leaves with a hint of indumentum when young, it bears mid-spring trusses of 13-15 funnel-shaped blooms that are pale yellow-pink, flushed and edged with pink. Zone 6.

'Petticoats' A small to medium-sized, densely foliaged bush with deep green leaves and flowers of a bright clear yellow. They are slightly frilled and funnel-shaped, in trusses of between nine and 13 blooms, opening in mid-spring. Excellent drainage is important. Zone 6.

'Pineapple Delight' Of the same parentage as 'Paprika Spiced' but a very different plant. It is a small to medium-sized mound of deep green, slightly puckered leaves with bright yellow, deepening with age, funnel-shaped flowers, in trusses of 12-14 blooms. Zone 7.

'Pink Pearl' Now over 100 years old, this classic large, pink-flowered rhododendron still sets the standard by which others are judged. It has mid-green leaves and conical trusses of between 11 and 15 funnel-shaped mid-pink blooms opening from deep pink buds and fading to pale pink. Zone 6.

'P.J. Mezitt' (syn 'P.J.M.') This American hybrid, introduced in the mid-1960s, is notable for its extreme hardiness, its bronze-green foliage which turns a rich purple-brown in winter and masses of lavender-purple flowers in early spring. Zone 4.

'Point Defiance' Of the same parentage as 'Lem's Monarch' and virtually identical in all respects, this is a large bush with rounded leaves and upright

Above: *Rhododendron* 'Pineapple Delight'
Below: *Rhododendron* 'President Roosevelt', one of the few rhododendrons with variegated foliage.

Rhododendron 'Purple Heart'

trusses of around 17 white, funnel-shaped flowers with deep pink to red edges. Zone 6.

'President Roosevelt' This is an old Dutch hybrid, medium-sized and still one of the few variegated foliage rhododendrons. The 4-6 in (10-15 cm) long leaves are deep green with a central yellow splash. The flowers are funnel-shaped and white, edged and flushed with red. They open early and are carried in conical trusses of five to 11 blooms. Zone 7.

'Princess Alice' Probably the most compact and least rangy of the old *R. edgeworthii* hybrids, 'Princess Alice' dates from 1860. It has fragrant pink flushed with white flowers in loose clusters and rather fuzzy foliage. Zone 9.

'Purple Gem' This small American hybrid, crossed by Gable of azalea fame and introduced in the 1950s, has an alpine-style growth habit with wiry twigs, tiny blue-green leaves and masses of small purple flowers. Zone 4.

Rhododendron 'Purple Gem'

'Purple Heart' A large shrub, similar in shape and foliage to its parent 'Purple Splendor', with flowers that are violet to purple with yellow-green throats. The upright conical trusses hold between six and 11 blooms and open mid-spring. Zone 6.

'Purple Splendor' Still one of the best purple-flowered rhododendrons, this *R. ponticum* hybrid was raised before 1900. It has narrow, slightly glossy, dark green leaves and the flowers, which open mid-spring on trusses of seven to 14 blooms, are deep purple with a near-black blotch. Zone 6.

'Rainbow' Similar in flower to 'Lem's Monarch' and 'Point Defiance', this large, upright shrub has glossy, rather narrow leaves and pink flowers edged with white carried on large trusses that sometimes droop under their own weight. It blooms in mid-spring. Zone 7.

'Razorbill' This small Scottish-raised shrub has little, bright green, rounded leaves and small tubular flowers in a glowing pink shade. An ideal rockery or alpine garden plant. Zone 7.

'Ring of Fire' A dense, medium-sized bush with mid-green leaves and slightly bronze new growth. The flowers are a striking bright yellow, flushed and edged orange-red. Funnel-shaped, they open mid-spring and are in trusses of five to 11 blooms. Zone 6.

'Rubicon' This densely foliaged, medium-sized bush has lush, somewhat puckered, glossy, deep green leaves. Its flowers open mid-spring and are funnel-shaped, a deep rich red and carried in trusses of up to 17 blooms. Zone 7.

'Sappho' Raised before 1847 but still distinctive and popular. When not in flower it looks much like any other large rhododendron, but in bloom its pure white flowers with a large, sharply contrasting, blackish purple flare can't be mistaken. The flowers are funnel-shaped and carried in upright conical trusses of between five and 11 blooms. Zone 5.

'Scarlet King' This large shrub was raised by Edgar Stead, better known for his Ilam azaleas. Showing its *R. griersonianum* heritage in its long, narrow, pointed leaves, it has a reputation for doing well in warm climates. As the name suggests, the flowers, massed in large trusses, are bright scarlet. Zone 7.

Rhododendron 'Senora Meldon'

'Scarlet Wonder' One of the best dwarf rhododendrons, this spreading *R. forrestii* hybrid has a dense covering of lush, deep green, rounded leaves and from mid-spring is smothered in deep red, bell-shaped flowers in loose clusters of four to seven blooms. Zone 5.

'Senora Meldon' Rather like a superior 'Blue Diamond' (one of its parents), this medium-sized shrub has narrow leaves that bronze in winter and in spring it produces loose clusters of mildly scented, light purple flowers with conspicuous stamens. Zone 7.

'Seta' Usually the first of the large-flowered rhododendrons to bloom, 'Seta' has blue-green pointed leaves and develops into an open, medium-sized bush. Its flowers, which are tubular to bell-shaped and in small clusters, are pale pink with a darker edge. Zone 7.

'Shamrock' This dwarf, densely foliaged bush has bright green leaves that develop purple tints in temperate winters. Its funnel-shaped flowers are an unusual yellow-green, smothering the plant from early spring in lax heads of three to nine blooms. It is hardy to Zone 6 but damaged by late frosts.

'Snow Lady' Dwarf to medium-sized, this bush has delightful bright green, fuzzy foliage as well as a brilliant show of loose clusters of slightly fragrant, white to cream, funnel-shaped flowers in early spring. Zone 6.

'Snow White' This small yakushimanum hybrid should not be confused with the much larger Kewense or Loderi plant of the same name. It forms a low mound of deep green foliage that in mid-spring is topped with pink flushed with white flowers that open from deep pink buds. Zone 7.

'Sonata' A spreading, medium-sized bush that becomes a dense mass of narrow, deep green leaves. It blooms late with rounded trusses of orange-red blooms with unusual and distinctive lavender to light red-purple edges. Zone 6.

'Sunup Sundown' A small, spreading bush with a dense covering of glossy green leaves. The name comes from the way the trusses of about 10 flowers change color, opening deep pink from red buds and fading to pale pink with hints of soft orange. Zone 7.

'Taurus' The drooping foliage of this large bush shows the influence of *R. strigillosum*. In addition to impressive leaves, it carries large buds through winter that in mid-spring open into large trusses of deep red, bell-shaped flowers with black-red spotting. Zone 6.

'Ted's Orchid Sunset' A stunning medium-sized bush with large, matt, mid-green leaves and bronze new growth. The funnel-shaped flowers, over 3 in (8 cm) wide and in trusses of seven to 11 blooms, open mid-spring in a dazzling combination of deep lavender-pink shaded orange, with orange-bronze throat markings. Zone 6.

'The Honourable Jean-Marie de Montague' Beautiful in its own right and with probably the longest name of any rhododendron, this hybrid is itself the parent of many fine plants. It has narrow, extremely dark green leaves and mid-spring flowers that set the standard for red. They are true blood red, funnel-shaped and in trusses of 10 to 14 blooms. Zone 6.

'Top Banana' In many ways a superior form of 'Hotei', one of its parents, this small bush has matt green foliage and masses of bright yellow flowers in mid-spring. Good drainage is important. Zone 7.

'Trewithen Orange' Resembling *R. cinnabarinum* in growth habit and foliage, this large shrub has rounded, glossy, leathery leaves and very distinctive, flared, tubular, orange flowers in loose clusters. Zone 6.

'Trude Webster' A large shrub that is almost worth growing for its foliage alone. It has rounded mid-

Rhododendron 'Taurus'

Above: *Rhododendron* 'Sonata'

Rhododendron 'Trewithen Orange'

green leaves and from mid-spring covers itself in huge trusses of 15-20 large, funnel-shaped, clear mid-pink flowers. Zone 5.

'Unique' While the changing flower colors of this medium-sized shrub are no longer as unusual as when it was introduced around 1930, 'Unique' is still a beautiful and desirable plant. It has slightly glossy, rounded leaves and from mid-spring its bright pink buds begin to open into trusses of pink, flushed pale yellow, funnel-shaped blooms that fade to cream. Zone 6.

'Van Nes Sensation' A large shrub with bright mid-green leaves. It blooms in mid-spring with trusses of seven to 11 large, slightly fragrant, funnel-shaped, white suffused with pink blooms opening from deep pink buds. Zone 6.

'Viennese Waltz' This Canadian-raised 'Lem's Cameo' hybrid is medium-sized with large leaves and impressive trusses of mildly fragrant cream flowers with a broad pink edge. It blooms mid-spring. Zone 6.

'Virginia Richards' A neat small to medium-sized bush with mid-green, pointed, elliptical leaves. Its orange buds open from mid-spring into funnel-shaped, red-blotched apricot flowers with soft creamy orange centers. The compact trusses hold between nine and 13 blooms. Zone 6.

Vireya rhododendrons

Also known as Malesian or Malaysian rhododendrons, the tropical vireyas number around 250 species, many of which are natural epiphytes from high rainfall areas of Southeast Asia through Borneo and New Guinea to northeast Australia. They tend to be rather straggly plants but make up for their untidy growth habit with very brightly colored and often fragrant flowers, mostly in loose heads of between five and nine blooms. Vireyas are not strictly seasonal in their blooming, though flowers are most likely in late summer and fall. Many vireyas are high altitude plants and will tolerate prolonged exposure to relatively cool temperatures, but few can withstand any frost. In mild, frost-free climates vireyas can be treated much like any other rhododendron, but in colder areas they are best grown in containers, using a coarse all-purpose potting mix with added humus. Feed occasionally with mild liquid fertilizers. Vireyas tend to be top-heavy, so make sure the pots can't tip over. In greenhouses it is often better to plant them in beds or troughs rather than individual pots. All the listed plants are Zone 10.

'Candy' Very like *R. jasminiflorum* and possibly a cultivated form of that species, 'Candy' has rounded mid-green leaves, a neat growth habit and fragrant, pale pink, tubular flowers.

'Flamenco Dancer' The widely flared, tubular, funnel-shaped flowers of this *R. aurigeranum* x *R. macgregoriae* hybrid are a soft but bright yellow. It is an upright bush with dark green, elliptical leaves.

'Gilded Sunrise' An upright, open shrub with bright golden yellow, tubular, funnel-shaped flowers that darken with age.

'Golden Charm' This compact hybrid has deep bronze-green, elliptical leaves and masses of large trusses of bright orange, tubular, funnel-shaped flowers.

'Whisperingrose' This American hybrid is very like what one would expect considering its parentage (*R. williamsianum* x 'Elizabeth'): a small bush with somewhat rounded, deep green foliage and pinkish red, bell-shaped flowers in clusters. Zone 6.

'White Pearl' (syn 'Halopeanum') A fast-growing, large shrub with deep green foliage and tall, conical trusses of pale pink flowers that fade to white. Although largely superseded by better plants, it is still widely grown for its extreme vigor. Flowers mid-spring. Zone 7.

'Winsome' This small to medium-sized bush is attractive throughout the year with bronze new growth and deep green, pointed leaves that have a pale buff indumentum. From mid-spring the foliage disappears under clusters of deep pink, bell-shaped flowers. Zone 7.

'Yaku Sunrise' Registered by Lancaster of the United States in 1967, this small *R. yakushimanum* hybrid produces deep pink flowers edged with white from mid-spring. It is a neat, densely foliaged, small bush that is considerably wider than it is high. Zone 6.

'Pink Delight' An old hybrid of unknown parentage, 'Pink Delight' has vivid pink, tubular, funnel-shaped flowers, an upright, rather open, growth habit and is the parent of several modern hybrids.

'Simbu Sunset' In common with many other vireyas with orange and yellow flowers, this compact plant with red-stemmed new growth has *R. laetum* x *R. zoelleri* parentage. The blooms are large with orange tubes, five deep orange lobes and yellow centers.

'Tropic Glow' Another *R. laetum* x *R. zoelleri* hybrid with golden yellow-edged orange-red flowers, in trusses of four and six blooms. It is a fairly tidy grower with large elliptical leaves.

Deciduous azaleas

Deciduous azaleas are really quite different from the other rhododendrons. They generally perform best in sunny locations, flower predominantly in yellow and orange shades, not pink, red or mauve and, of course, they lose all their foliage in the fall. Most are very hardy and many develop intense fall foliage colors.

Deciduous azalea hybrids are divided into groups based on their parentage. The main groups, along with descriptions of a few of the most popular cultivars, are as follows.

Ghent

In the early 1800s Ghent, Belgium, was the main center for azalea breeding. The earliest hybrids were raised from *R. calendulaceum*, *R. nudiflorum*, *R. luteum* and *R. viscosum*. Later, *R. molle* was crossed with *R. viscosum* to produce the Viscosepalum hybrids, which have now largely disappeared. Further developments include the double Ghent or Rustica strain. These plants, introduced from the late 1850s, were followed in 1890 by a similar group of double-flowered hybrids known as Rustica Flore Pleno hybrids.

Ghent azaleas tend to be large, late-flowering plants with small flowers in large heads. They are

Rhododendron 'Flamenco Dancer', a vireya.

often fragrant and all are hardy to Zone 6. At the height of their popularity, over 500 Ghent cultivars were available. Today they have been mainly superseded by later styles.

'Coccinea Speciosa' Bright orange-pink flowers with a striking orange blotch.

'Daviesii' A tall, upright, Viscosepalum hybrid with fragrant white to pale yellow flowers late in the season.

'Nancy Waterer' Large, bright yellow, scented flowers from late spring.

'Narcissiflora' A tall, upright hybrid with small, double, fragrant, pale yellow flowers from late spring.

'Norma' A Rustica Flore Pleno hybrid with small, pink-edged orange-red, double flowers.

'Phebe' (syn 'Phoebe') A Rustica Flore Pleno hybrid with deep yellow, double flowers.

'Vulcan' An upright bush with deep red flowers that have an orange-yellow blotch.

Mollis

The mollis azaleas were developed in Belgium and Holland from Ghent azaleas. They show a greater *R. molle* influence than the Ghents and some may actually be forms of *R. molle* var *japonicum* rather than hybrids. They first appeared in the late 1860s and were further refined over the next 30 years.

Mollis azaleas flower from mid-spring and are usually over 6 ft (1.8 m) tall. The flowers are larger than the Ghents, tend to be bright yellow, orange or red and they are all singles. All are hardy to Zone 7 and most will grow in Zone 6.

Because mollis azaleas can be difficult to propagate by cuttings, this group includes seedling strains. These reproduce reasonably true to type but it is best to choose your plants when in flower, because any label description is likely to be an approximation only.

'Anthony Koster' Bright yellow flowers with a vivid orange blotch.

'Apple Blossom' Light pink flowers fading to nearly white.

'Christopher Wren' Large, bright yellow flowers with an orange blotch.

'Cockatoo' Orange-yellow flowers with a darker blotch.

'Floradora' Bright orange flowers with a red blotch.

'J.C. van Tol' Apricot-pink flowers with an orange blotch.

Deciduous azalea 'Antony Koster', a mollis hybrid.

'Orange Glow' Developed from 'J.C. van Tol', this hybrid has apricot flowers with an orange blotch.

'Spek's Orange' A relatively small bush with very large, orange-blotched red flowers in trusses of up to nine blooms.

'Winston Churchill' Orange-red flowers with a red blotch.

Occidentale

Rhododendron occidentale is a fragrant, white- to pink-flowered, deciduous azalea from the west coast of the United States. It was discovered in 1827 and entered cultivation in the 1850s.

Occidentale hybrids are among the most fragrant azaleas and usually develop into large plants, although they are quite slow growing. They bloom from mid-spring and have flowers up to 3 in (8 cm) in diameter. The flowers are white or pale pink, often with conspicuous golden throat markings.

'Delicatissima' Scented, creamy, white flushed with pink flowers with a yellow blotch.

'Exquisita' Frilled, highly scented, white flushed with pink flowers with an orange-yellow blotch.

'Leonard Frisbie' Very large, fragrant, frilled flowers that are white suffused with pink with a yellow flare.

'Magnifica' Purple-red flowers with a gold blotch.

'Pistil Packin' Mama' An unusual form from Oregon in which the flowers are reduced to just the pistil and a small socket at its base.

'Stagecoach Cream' Flowers creamy white with large, orange-yellow upper petals. Propagated originally from a plant found in Humboldt County, California.

Knap Hill, Exbury & Ilam

The Knap Hill, Exbury and Ilam hybrids are the most widely grown deciduous azaleas. The original plants were developed from about 1870 at the Knap Hill, England, nursery of Anthony Waterer. Starting with Ghent azaleas, he crossbred extensively and selected only the best of the resultant hybrids. Waterer named only one of his plants, 'Nancy Waterer' (officially a Ghent hybrid) and it was not until the seedlings were acquired by Sunningdale Nurseries in 1924 that plants started to be made available to the public.

Deciduous azalea 'Exquisita'.

Lionel de Rothschild of Exbury developed the Exbury strain from Knap Hill seedlings. The first of these, 'Hotspur', was introduced in 1934. The collection was almost lost during the Second World War and relatively few hybrids were introduced until the 1950s.

Edgar Stead of Ilam, Christchurch, New Zealand, working with various species and Ghent and Knap Hill hybrids, further refined the strain. Stead's work was continued by Dr. J.S. Yeates.

Most are large bushes with vividly colored single flowers. Hardiness varies, though most are hardy to Zone 6.

'Brazil' An Exbury hybrid. Bright orange-red flowers.

'Cannon's Double' A low-growing Exbury hybrid. Light yellow and cream double flowers.

'Carmen' (syn 'Ilam Carmen') An early-flowering Ilam hybrid. Apricot flowers with a yellow-orange blotch.

'Cecile' An Exbury hybrid. Red flowers with an orange blotch.

'**Chaffinch**' A Knap Hill hybrid. Deep pink flowers. Often sold as seedlings and quite variable.

'**Gallipoli**' An Exbury hybrid. Apricot-pink flower with an orange blotch.

'**Giant Orange**' Ilam. As the name suggests, it has large orange flowers.

'**Gibraltar**' An Exbury hybrid. Bright orange-red flowers from mid-spring.

'**Homebush**' A Knap Hill hybrid. Semi-double purplish red flowers.

'**Hotspur**' An Exbury hybrid. Bright orange-red flowers.

'**Klondyke**' An Exbury hybrid. Bright orange flowers with an orange-yellow blotch.

'**Louie Williams**' (syn 'Ilam Louis Williams') An Ilam hybrid. Large, light pink and soft yellow flowers with an orange blotch.

'**Maori**' A low-growing Ilam hybrid. Bright orange-red flowers in large trusses.

'**Ming**' (syn 'Ilam Ming') An Ilam hybrid. Large orange flowers with a yellow blotch. Among the first to flower.

'**Persil**' A Knap Hill hybrid. White with a soft yellow blotch.

'**Red Rag**' An Ilam hybrid. Slightly frilled, bright orange-red flowers.

'**Strawberry Ice**' An Exbury hybrid. Yellowish pink flushed with mid-pink flowers with an orange blotch.

'**Wallowa Red**' A Yeates Ilam hybrid. Deep red flowers overlaid with orange. Brilliant red fall foliage.

Deciduous azalea 'Ming' (syn. 'Ilam Ming').

'**Yellow Giant**' (syn 'Ilam Yellow Giant') An Ilam hybrid. Very large, bright yellow flowers.

Other groups

Many American hybridizers have raised deciduous azaleas, but often with only localized distribution. The Carlson hybrids, for example, are popular in the northeast where they were developed, while some Oregon garden centers stock the local Slonecker hybrids, and in Georgia you'll find the Beasleys. The Girard hybrids are probably still the best known of these groups, but recently the University of Minnesota's Northern Lights hybrids have become very popular and are now widely distributed.

Northern Lights Hybrids

Developed with extreme hardiness in mind at the university's Landscape Arboretum, these azaleas are all capable of surviving −35°F (−37°C). They are

compact for deciduous azaleas, growing to around 5-6 ft (1.5-1.8 m) high and wide.

'Apricot Surprise' The flowers are a combination of yellow, apricot and orange tones on a compact plant.

'Golden Lights' A super-hardy, vigorous, mildew-resistant, spreading bush with fragrant, bright yellow flowers.

'Lemon Lights' Bright lemon-yellow flowers.

'Mandarin Lights' Lightly scented, ruffled, orange-red flowers on a neat, rounded bush.

'Northern Hi-Lights' Cream flowers with a yellow flare. A compact, mildew-resistant plant with bronze new growth.

'Orchid Lights' Starry, deep pink, sterile flowers. A very compact plant and the hardiest of the Northern Lights hybrids.

'Rosy Lights' Fragrant deep pink flowers shaded with even darker pink on an upright, spreading bush.

'Spicy Lights' Mildly fragrant, light orange flowers with a darker flare. Compact and well-branched.

'White Lights' Fragrant white flowers with a yellow blotch. A vigorous, upright bush.

Girard Hybrids

Developed mainly from Knap Hill azaleas and raised by Peter E. Girard of Geneva, Ohio, who also produced evergreen azaleas, this range includes many double flowers and vivid fall foliage colors. All are hardy to Zone 5 and most grow to around 6-8 ft (1.8-2.4 m) tall. The names are sometimes prefaced with 'Girard's', but that is not part of their registered names.

'Crimson Tide' Double, deep red flowers tightly packed in large trusses.

'Orange Jolly' Large, double, orange flowers in ball-shaped trusses. The flowers are sterile and do not set seed.

'Pink Delight' Bright pink, fragrant, hose-in-hose blooms in trusses of up to 24 flowers. Tall.

'Red Pom Pom' Large, double, fragrant, red blooms in large, tightly packed trusses on a compact bush.

'Salmon Delight' Bright yellow flowers flushed with rose pink. Up to 30 flowers per truss on a large, spreading bush.

'Yellow Pom Pom' Large, double, fragrant, bright yellow flowers in tight heads.

Evergreen azaleas

Evergreen azaleas occur naturally in Japan, China, Korea and the cooler parts of Southeast Asia and, despite the name, are semi-deciduous. They have two types of leaf: light-textured, often larger spring

Evergreen azalea 'Pink Dream', a Belgian Indica.

leaves and the tougher, more leathery, fall growth. The spring foliage is shed in the fall but the summer leaves are largely retained over winter. Although with age many reach 6 ft (1.8 m) tall, they tend to be small to medium-sized shrubs.

Evergreen azaleas are divided into groups based on their parentage. The following is a very brief outline of the main groups with descriptions of a few of the most popular cultivars in each.

Indica

The first Indica hybrids were developed in Belgium in the 1850s as houseplants. Their main parent is *Rhododendron simsii*, which often produces bicolor flowers and is easily forced into bloom in the winter. Indicas are the fanciest azaleas with an enormous range of frilly doubles and multi-color flowers. Mostly around 24 x 36 in (60 cm tall by 90 cm wide),

some can reach 4 ft (1.2 m) tall or more. They are generally hardy to Zone 9 and a few survive in Zone 8, though most Indicas will be badly damaged if regularly exposed to 21°F (−6°C) or colder.

There are several sub-groups, such as Kerrigan and Rutherford Indicas. Many are very similar and simply represent various breeders' efforts along the same lines.

Belgian Indicas

'Albert Elizabeth' Semi-double white flowers with a broad, deep pink edge. Early-flowering.

'Coconut Ice' Variable single to semi-double, pale pink flowers with darker shading and edges. Flowers early to mid-spring.

'Comtesse de Kerchove' Light apricot-pink, double flowers with orange-pink shading. An early-flowering, low-growing bush with light green foliage. Relatively hardy.

'Deutsche Perle' A very early, pure white, double flower. Trim annually to keep the bush compact.

'Elsa Kaerger' Semi-double, deep orange-red flowers from mid-spring. A really vibrant color.

'Gerhardt Nicolai' Very large, deep pink, semi-double to double flowers. It blooms early and the foliage has a tendency to sunburn.

'Goyet' Capable of growing to 4 ft (1.2 m) tall, it has very large, frilled, dark red, double flowers. Blooms from early spring.

'Hexe' Blooming from mid-spring and relatively hardy. Deep green foliage and vivid, purple-red, slightly ruffled, hose-in-hose flowers. The blooms are small but profuse.

'Leopold Astrid' Early, white, double flowers with red edges. Magnificent in full bloom and also has good foliage.

'**Little Girl**' Frilled, light pink, hose-in-hose flowers in mid-spring. A heavy-flowering compact bush.

'**Mme Alfred Sander**' A neat, compact bush with dark foliage and very well-shaped, formal, double, deep purplish-pink flowers in early spring.

'**Orchid Gem**' A medium-sized shrub with single, ruffled, purple flowers with darker markings from early spring. Very quick-growing.

'**Paul Schaeme**' An old cultivar that has been very influential in the development of modern forcing azaleas. It has masses of double, bright red flowers from early spring.

'**Pink Dream**' A medium-sized shrub with large, single flowers in a rich mid-pink shade with a darker blotch. It flowers from early to mid-spring.

'**Pink Ice**' Early-flowering, semi-double, pale pink flowers with occasional deep pink flecks and stripes are at their best just before fully open. Low, spreading growth habit.

'**Red Poppy**' This upright bush has very distinctive single to semi-double, deep red, poppy-shaped flowers and is one of the first azaleas to bloom.

'**Red Wing**' A fairly hardy, spreading bush with deep purple-red, hose-in-hose flowers from early spring. It is a strong grower when young.

'**Rosa Belton**' Single, white flowers with a broad lavender edge. This heavy-flowering bush blooms early and has hairy, light green foliage.

'**Southern Aurora**' Double, white flowers, heavily flushed and edged orange-red. About as close to true orange as you'll find in an evergreen azalea. It is spectacular and never fails to attract attention.

'**Vervaeneana**' Compact and early flowering with double, soft pink flowers with a deep reddish blotch

Evergreen azalea 'Orchard Gem', a Belgian Indica.

and white borders. Raised in 1886 and the parent of several sports.

'**Violacea**' This upright grower can become a large, spreading bush with age. It has semi-double, magenta-purple flowers from early spring. Trim to shape when young.

Southern Indicas

Not long after the Belgian Indicas became popular in Europe they reached the United States. Most were too tender to be used as anything but houseplants in the north. However, in the milder south many acres were planted by plantation owners. With time, the azaleas set seed, some of which germinated. Some of these seedlings were cultivated as new varieties and were in turn bred with the surviving cultivars to produce the Southern Indicas.

The Southern Indicas of today are a mixed bag: old Belgian Indicas, chance seedlings perpetuated and deliberately bred hybrids. As a group they are usually hardier to both sun and frost than the Belgians and tend to be larger plants when mature.

'**Fielder's White**' A large, spreading shrub that is often used as a background or filler. It has narrow, light green leaves and slightly fragrant, single, white flowers from mid-spring. Remove any branches with mauve flowers as they may come to predominate. Zone 8.

'Mardi Gras' A small, shrubby plant with semi-double, orange-pink flowers with broad white edging. Blooms early to mid-spring. Zone 9.

'Modele' A small, spreading, heavy-flowering shrub with deep purple-red, double flowers from mid-spring. Zone 8.

Rutherford Indicas

These hybrids were developed in the United States, in the 1920s, as greenhouse forcing plants and as such they are very similar to Belgian Indicas. The name Rutherford comes from the Bobbink and Atkins Nursery of East Rutherford, New Jersey, where the hybrids were developed.

'Alaska' A medium-sized bush bearing white flowers with a light green blotch that vary on one plant from single to almost full double. Zone 9.

'Dorothy Gish' Mid-spring blooming with frilled hose-in-hose flowers of an unusual orange-pink shade with a darker blotch. An attractive small bush. Zone 8.

'Purity' A small, early to mid-spring blooming bush with double, white flowers and deep green foliage. Zone 8.

'Rose Queen' Semi-double, mid-pink flowers with darker markings from early spring. A low, spreading bush. Zone 8.

Kerrigan Indicas

In effect just another form of the Belgian Indica. Bred in the United States from the 1950s onwards, principally as greenhouse plants. Most are fairly frost tender when young but they do have very showy flowers. Hardy to the warmest parts of Zone 8.

Evergreen azalea 'Gay Paree', a Kerrigan Indica.

'Bride's Bouquet' A medium-sized bush with beautiful, formal, rosebud, double white flowers with greenish throat markings. Opening mid-spring, the blooms need some shade if they are to last.

'Gay Paree' A small bush with spectacular bicolor, semi-double, white flowers with deep pink edges. It blooms mid-spring.

'Ripples' An extremely heavy-flowering, small bush with ruffled, double, deep purple-pink flowers that open from early spring.

Indicum and Mucronatum hybrids

Hybrids between *Rhododendron indicum*, *R. simsii* and *R. ripense*, these plants are usually quite large and have sticky, light green leaves and white or mauve scented flowers.

'Alba Magnifica' A medium to large shrub with single yellow flowers marked with white, which open mid-spring and are slightly fragrant. Zone 8.

'Balsaminaeflora' A small bush with very fully double, rosebud-style flowers in an orange-pink shade. It blooms from early spring and may be trimmed as a low hedge. Zone 8.

Evergreen azalea, the Kerrigan Indica hybrid 'Ripples'.

'Magnifica Rosea' (syn. 'Magnifica') A medium-sized shrub with single mid-pink to mauve flowers that are slightly fragrant and open mid-spring. Zone 8.

'Salmonea' A medium-sized shrub with single, deep salmon-pink flowers with darker markings. Plants sold as 'Splendens' or 'Salmonea Splendens' appear identical. May be trimmed as a hedge. Zone 9.

Kurume

Kurume, on Kyushu, the southernmost main island of Japan, has long been a major azalea growing area. In 1919 the famous plant collector Ernest Wilson visited Kurume and obtained examples of 50 cultivars, which he introduced to Western gardens as Wilson's Fifty. Since then many further hybrids have been raised and introduced.

Kurume azaleas clearly show the influence of *Rhododendron kiusianum*, a species that grows wild on Mt. Kirishima. They are dense, compact growers with small leaves and masses of small flowers early in the season. Many Kurume azaleas have hose-in-hose flowers in which the sepals become petal-like and create the effect of a second corolla.

Most are best grown in sun or very light shade. They respond well to trimming after flowering and are generally hardy to Zone 7.

'Addy Wery' A medium-sized bush with deep orange-red single flowers and bronze winter foliage color.

'Blaauw's Pink' Early, light salmon pink, hose-in-hose flowers with a darker throat. A small, spreading bush that benefits from pruning to keep it compact.

'Christmas Cheer' (syn. 'Ima Shojo') A medium-sized shrub with small, rounded, bright green leaves and masses of tiny, vivid cerise-red, hose-in-hose flowers. May be trimmed as a hedge. No. 36 of Wilson's Fifty.

'Fairy Queen' (syn. 'Aioi') A small shrub with pale apricot-pink, hose-in-hose flowers with a red blotch. No. 43 of Wilson's Fifty.

'Hinode Giri' A medium-sized, heavily foliaged shrub that produces masses of tiny, cerise-red, single flowers. No. 42 of Wilson's Fifty.

'Iroha Yama' (syn. 'Dainty') A dense, medium-sized shrub with small, bright green, rounded leaves and single white flowers that have deep apricot-pink edges. No. 8 of Wilson's Fifty.

'Kirin' (syn. 'Coral Bells') Probably the most popular azalea of all, 'Kirin' is a dense, heavily foliaged, medium-sized bush with rounded, bright green leaves that become bronze in winter. From very early spring it becomes a solid mass of soft pastel pink, hose-in-hose flowers. No. 22 of Wilson's Fifty.

'Mother's Day' (syn. 'Muttertag') A Kurume that is treated like an Indica and is widely used as a forcing plant. It is a medium-sized bush with vivid, cerise-red, hose-in-hose or semi-double flowers.

Evergreen azalea 'Sui Yohi', a Kurume cultivar.

'**Osaraku**' (syn. 'Penelope') Single flowers with very delicate shadings of white suffused with light purple. A medium-sized shrub, very dense and twiggy with tiny leaves. No. 17 of Wilson's Fifty.

'**Red Robin**' (syn. 'Waka Kayede') This small, spreading bush positively glows with single, bright orange-red flowers from mid-spring. It benefits from trimming to shape when young. No. 38 of Wilson's Fifty.

'**Sui Yohi**' (syn. 'Sprite') An exquisite bloom, delicately shaded and textured. The flower is single, white, flushed pale pink with pink petal tips. The bush is medium to large, benefits from trimming when young and is one of the more frost-tender Kurumes. No. 10 of Wilson's Fifty.

'**Ward's Ruby**' Usually regarded as the evergreen azalea with the deepest red flowers, this medium-sized, upright, twiggy bush has small, single flowers with great intensity of color. Somewhat frost tender.

Amoenum Kurumes

These plants are very much in the Kurume style. The well-known 'Amoena' is a form of the plant formerly known as *Rhododendron obtusum*, which is itself now regarded as a hybrid of *R. sataense*, *R. kiusianum* and *R. kaempferi*.

'**Amoena**' This medium to large shrub is always a feature of early spring due to its tremendously prolific display of tiny, purple, hose-in-hose flowers. It becomes a solid block of color. It is extremely tough and makes a good hedge even in exposed positions. Zone 6.

'**Princess Maude**' A large, twiggy bush with rather open growth and small, vivid, deep pink flowers from early spring. It benefits from trimming when young. Zone 8.

Kaempferi

Kaempferis are derived from *Rhododendron kaempferi* and *R. yedoense*, both of which withstand temperatures down to −20°C (−5°F). However, when exposed to very low temperatures, they drop most of their foliage.

Bred mainly in the United States and Holland, primarily with hardiness in mind, many of the newer hybrids have quite fancy flowers. Kaempferis often develop red foliage tints in winter and tend to have simple, very brightly colored flowers. All are hardy to at least Zone 6.

'Blue Danube' A medium-sized bush with light green foliage and deep purple-pink flowers in mid-spring.

'Double Beauty' A small bush with light green foliage, low spreading growth and deep purple-pink, hose-in-hose flowers from early spring.

'Johanna' A medium to large shrub with deep red, single to semi-double flowers from mid-spring. Bright purple-red fall and winter foliage color.

'John Cairns' A medium to large bush with small, bright orange-red, single flowers.

Vuyk hybrids

Developed from 1921 by Vuyk Van Nes Nursery of Boskoop, Holland. These hybrids are very like the original Kaempferis. Zone 6.

'Florida' A small to medium-sized shrub with light red, hose-in-hose flowers from mid-spring. Neat and compact if trimmed when young.

'Palestrina' White to pale cream, single flowers with yellow-green spotting. A compact, medium-sized, free-flowering bush with bright green foliage.

'Queen Wilhelmina' A large, spreading bush with long, narrow, lance-shaped leaves and large, single, orange-red flowers with a black-red blotch from late mid-spring.

'Vuyk's Scarlet' A small bush with masses of large, single, bright red flowers from early spring. Always impressive and reliably evergreen even under adverse conditions.

Evergreen azalea 'Caroline Gable'

Gable hybrids

These hybrids, developed by Joseph Gable of Pennsylvania, were bred with hardiness as a prime objective. Not only was this achieved but some quite showy double flowers were also raised. Most are hardy to Zone 7 or the milder parts of Zone 6.

'Caroline Gable' A small to medium-sized bush with deep purple-pink, hose-in-hose flowers from mid-spring. Very heavy-flowering and often has excellent winter foliage color.

'Isabel' This medium-sized bush has simple, single, mauve flowers from mid-spring. Its attraction lies not in the individual blooms, but in their profusion.

'Purple Splendor' A small, spreading bush with narrow leaves and frilled, light purple, hose-in-hose flowers from mid-spring.

'Rosebud' A tough and colorful medium-sized bush with very fully double, bright mid-pink flowers from mid-spring.

Girard hybrids

Developed in the late 1940s by Peter Girard of Ohio, these are compact, hardy hybrids that are smaller than most Kaempferis. Zone 6.

'Girard's Border Gem' A dwarf, small-leafed bush with deep pink, single flowers from mid-spring.

'Girard's Chiara' A dwarf bush with ruffled, deep cerise, hose-in-hose flowers with a reddish blotch. Blooms mid-spring.

Shammarello hybrids

These bushes are similar to the Gable hybrids; indeed many have Gable parentage. They are very tough and usually hardy to Zone 5.

'Desiree' A strong, medium-sized, spreading bush with frilled, single, white flowers from early spring.

'Elsie Lee' A medium-sized bush with semi-double to double, mauve flowers with darker markings from mid-spring. An attractive flower in an unusual shade.

Satsuki

Most gardeners regard the Kurumes as the traditional Japanese azaleas. However, the Satsukis are more revered in Japan, though they are relatively new to Western gardens, which probably explains the confusion.

Satsuki means fifth month, and while not a direct reference to May, it does indicate that they are late-flowering. Because of this, Satsuki blooms need protection from the summer sun to last.

Satsukis have large, highly variable, single flowers. One plant can display a wide range of color and pattern in its flowers. They are generally small, spreading plants and are hardy to the mildest parts of Zone 7.

Evergreen azalea 'Daishuhai', a Satsuki hybrid.

'Benigasa' (Red Umbrella) A dwarf shrub with rounded, deep green leaves and large, single, deep orange-red flowers from late spring.

'Chinzan' (Rare Mountain) A dwarf, spreading bush with small leaves and single, bright pink flowers with a darker blotch, opening from mid-spring.

'Daishuhai' (Great Vermilion Cup) A small shrub with more open growth than most Satsukis, though by no means rangy. It has single, white flowers with a clearly defined red tip to each petal.

'Fancy', mid-pink flowers with white edges, pink markings and occasional pink flakes and sectors; **'Light Pink'**, pale pink flowers with darker markings; **'Salmon'**, frilled, bright salmon-pink flowers; **'White'**, heavily frilled, white flowers.

'Gumpo' (A Group of Phoenixes) There are many forms of 'Gumpo'. All are dwarf bushes that are smothered in single flowers from mid-spring. They are ideally suited to rockeries or small gardens.

'Hitoya No Haru' (Glory of Spring) Among the last azaleas to bloom, this dwarf shrub has glossy foliage and large, single, bright lavender-pink flowers.

'**Issho No Haru**' (Spring of a Lifetime) A dwarf, late-blooming shrub with large, single, soft pastel pink flowers with occasional purple splashes.

'**Shiko**' (Purple Light) This is a dwarf bush with very large, single, lavender-pink flowers from late spring. The flowers are highly variable and often have white or purple flakes and sectors.

'**Shugetsu**' (Autumn Moon) A medium-sized shrub with large, single, white flowers edged bright purple. The flowers are variable, with many patterns seen on one plant.

Inter-Group

This catch-all collection of sub-groups includes the hybrids produced by breeding between the other groups and also includes those raised from newly introduced species.

Glenn Dale hybrids

In 1935 B.Y. Morrison of the U.S. Department of Agriculture Plant Introduction Section at Glenn Dale, Maryland, started breeding azaleas in an attempt to produce hardy plants in a good color range and to fill a then existing mid-season gap in flowering.

Of the thousands of clones, most of the 440 selected were released in 1947-49 with the remainder following in 1952. Many are no longer common. Most are hardy to Zone 7.

Evergreen azalea 'Martha Hitchcock', a Glenn Dale hybrid.

'**Ben Morrison**' This medium to large shrub was raised by Morrison but not released by him. It was later introduced to commemorate his work. In mid-spring it has striking, single, deep rusty red flowers with darker markings and broad white edges.

'**Festive**' A medium to large bush with single, white flowers attractively flecked and striped with purple. It flowers early.

'**Glacier**' Single, white flowers tinted light green. It blooms from mid-spring and can become a large bush.

'**Martha Hitchcock**' A very tough and vigorous, medium-sized bush that from mid-spring bears large, single, white flowers with a broad purplish pink edge.

'**Vespers**' A medium-sized, early-flowering bush bearing single to semi-double white flowers with green markings and occasional pink splashes.

Evergreen azalea 'Ben Morrison', a Glenn Dale hybrid.

Evergreen azalea 'Anna Kehr', a hybrid from North Carolina.

Back Acres hybrids

Morrison produced these hybrids after his retirement from the U.S. Department of Agriculture. They are compact plants that are generally hardy to Zone 7.

'Bayou' A small to medium-sized bush that from early spring bears ruffled, single flowers that are white or very pale pink with darker flecks or sectors.

'Debonaire' A small shrub with bright pink, single flowers that have darker edges and a light center. It blooms mid-spring.

'Hearthglow' A medium-sized bush with unusual, camellia-like, double blooms in pink flushed with reddish orange, opening just after mid-spring.

'Miss Jane' A small bush bearing white double flowers with deep pink edges. Late flowering, it requires shade for the display to last.

'Whitehouse' A small, spreading bush with single white flowers marked in yellow-brown. It blooms in mid-spring.

August Kehr hybrids

Developed by another U.S. Department of Agriculture employee, Dr. August Kehr, these hybrids represent a lifetime's work. Kehr bred many plants but released only a handful of the hardiest and most beautiful. They are among the best evergreen azaleas for combining showy double flowers with hardiness.

'Anna Kehr' Very fully double, deep pink flowers from mid-spring on a small bush. 'Anna Kehr' often takes time to flower heavily and requires shaping when young but is well worth the effort. Zone 7.

'White Rosebud' A medium-sized bush with very fully double, white flowers with green throats. It blooms mid-spring and, for a white, is sun-tolerant. Zone 6.

Greenwood hybrids

Developed in Oregon by using Kurume, Glenn Dale and Gable hybrids, these very hardy plants are noted for doing well in cool climates. Most are compact bushes and hardy to Zone 6.

'Greenwood Orange' Masses of small, orange-red, double flowers from mid-spring. A small bush with a rather open growth habit that benefits from trimming to shape when young.

'Royal Robe' A dwarf, mound-forming bush with light purple, hose-in-hose flowers from mid-spring. Excellent for rockeries.

'Tenino' Deep pinkish-purple hose-in-hose flowers from mid-spring. Large blooms on a dwarf bush.

Harris hybrids

Developed by James Harris of Georgia from 1970 onwards, these plants are very compact, heavy-flowering and quite hardy once established.

'Fascination' A small bush with Satsuki-like, large, single flowers with a broad, deep red border and a white or pale pink center. Zone 7.

'Frosted Orange' A medium-sized, twiggy, spreading bush with white flowers that have a striking, broad, orange-red border. It is spectacular but blooms late and needs shade for the display to last. Zone 7.

'Miss Suzie' A small, low-growing, heavily foliaged bush with bright red, hose-in-hose flowers from mid-spring. Red winter foliage. Zone 6.

North Tisbury hybrids

When *Rhododendron nakaharai* came into cultivation, a new style of azalea made its appearance: the ground cover that could be adapted to hanging baskets. Polly Hill of Massachusetts pioneered these plants during the 1960s and '70s and produced low, mounding or trailing bushes grown as much for their form as for their blooms. Zone 6.

'Pink Pancake' This near-prostrate, spreading cultivar has small mid-pink flowers with red markings and blooms late. It is superb in rockeries or hanging baskets.

'Red Fountain' An excellent plant for spilling over banks or in hanging baskets, with simple, single, red flowers late in spring.

'Susannah Hill' This dwarf cultivar has red, hose-in-hose flowers that are sun tolerant, making it one of the best for exposed positions.

Nuccio hybrids

The Nuccios of California, perhaps better known for their camellias, also breed azaleas. They have used a wide range of material and, as a result, Nuccio hybrids cover the whole spectrum of flower type, size and hardiness.

'Bit of Sunshine' A small Kurume-style cultivar with masses of vivid pinkish red, hose-in-hose flowers from early spring. Zone 6.

'Happy Days' A small Indica-style cultivar with bright mid-purple, rosebud, double flowers from early spring. The flowers last well over a long season. Zone 8.

'Purple Glitters' A medium to large upright bush, this Kurume-style cultivar is smothered in vivid, purplish pink, single flowers from early spring. **'Rose Glitters'** is a deep cerise form. Zone 6.

Robin Hill hybrids

These hybrids were bred from 1937 to 1981 by Robert Gartrell of Wyckoff, New Jersey. From the 20,000 seedlings trialed he eventually released 69 cultivars. Most are medium-sized, relatively hardy shrubs.

'Betty Ann Voss' This low, spreading cultivar has late, semi-double to hose-in-hose, bright pink flowers and attractive glossy foliage. Zone 6.

'Early Beni' A small, mounding bush with semi-double, deep orange-red flowers from early spring. It is compact and sun-tolerant. Zone 7.

'Lady Louise' Semi-double to double apricot-pink flowers with reddish markings appear in mid-spring on a small, spreading bush with bronze winter foliage. Zone 7.

'Nancy of Robin Hill' A small bush bearing semi-double, light pink flowers with darker markings. It blooms from mid-spring. Zone 7.

'Watchet' This dwarf cultivar has single, mid-pink flowers with white throats and blooms from just after mid-spring. Zone 7.

'White Moon' A small, very Satsuki-like, spreading cultivar with large, single, white flowers in late spring. The flowers are occasionally splashed with pink and need shade to prevent burning. Zone 7.

CHAPTER 7

Planting

Planting is the final step. Prepare the site carefully, then plant properly and the rhododendrons will largely look after themselves.

It is very common for rhododendrons to grow well for a while, then to start dropping foliage, become yellow and die back. This can nearly always be traced back to root rot caused by poor drainage.

Azaleas 'Joga' and 'Mucronatum Alba' make an attractive foreground for Japanese maples.

The plants are fine until their roots hit the subsoil clay or reach the permanent water table. When that happens the roots can no longer spread to find nutrients and they may start to rot.

Regular feeding will keep such plants alive, but it isn't really a cure. The answer is a well-drained site and extra preparation, especially with larger-growing plants. It's all very well to prepare the top 20 in (50 cm) of soil for a 5 ft (1.5 m) high plant, but taller plants have larger and deeper root systems. Although rhododendrons are very shallow-rooted compared to most plants, a tree-sized specimen will still be anchored by a substantial root system.

Good drainage is best taken care of before planting time. Because you took the time to work in plenty of compost before planting, the drainage should be reasonably good, but check it just to make sure. Dig a 20 in (50 cm) deep hole and fill it with water. If the water disappears within four to six hours the drainage should be adequate. If after that time there is still water in the hole or if the hole fills with water as you dig it, you need to think about improving the drainage or planting in raised beds.

A raised bed can be a naturally higher part of the garden, an artificial mound or a boxed bed. If poor drainage is still a possibility or you have very hard clay subsoil, field drains may need to be laid. These should drain the soil to at least a depth of 3 ft (1 m). If you can go deeper, so much the better.

It is also a good idea to incorporate a mild all-purpose fertilizer prior to planting. Fresh animal manures and harsh chemical fertilizers can burn tender young roots so use mild fertilizers and make sure they are worked well into the soil.

Only when you are satisfied that the ground is thoroughly prepared is it time to plant. Newly

planted rhododendrons need loose soil in order to make quick root growth, so make sure you dig a hole that is at least twice the size of the plant's root ball.

Thoroughly soak the shrub before you remove it from its container or the roots may adhere to the sides and suffer damage. Plastic bags may be cut away or carefully eased off and pots usually come away cleanly if up-ended and given a firm rap on the rim. If the shrub appears pot bound, gently loosen up the root ball. Otherwise just lightly work your fingers into the root ball to allow moisture to penetrate and spread a few of the lower roots to get them growing in the right direction.

Place the rhododendron in the hole and check the soil level. It should be at the same level it was in the container. Gently firm the plant into position with your heel as you replace the soil but don't ram the earth back into place or you'll undo all the work that went into loosening it up.

Mulch around the plant and stake large rhododendrons to prevent wind rock. In dry areas or on sloping sites it is a good idea to make a rim of soil or mulch around new plants to act as a reservoir that can be filled when the plants are watered.

Gardens are more than just plants. The relationships they have with each other add an extra dimension as is shown by this grouping of *Rhododendron* 'Percy Wiseman' with the foliage of irises and *Artemisia* 'Valerie Finnis'.

Watering

Newly planted rhododendrons need ample moisture, but don't drown them. If the plant is slow to come into growth, yet you are watering and feeding, it may be that the root ball is still dry at the center. That is because most nurseries now raise their rhododendrons in containers of soil-less mix rather than growing them in the open ground and lifting them just prior to selling.

Potting mixes can be very difficult to re-wet once they have dried out. It is easy to think you are watering deeply when in reality the surface soil around the plant is getting wet while the all-important root ball remains dry.

The only way to check this is to probe around the roots. If those closest to the main stem are not noticeably dry, you may have to lift the plant to check the roots. This will also highlight any problems with root-feeding insects or root rot.

CHAPTER 8

Maintenance

Rhododendrons are very self-supporting but they still need occasional maintenance.

Weeding and mulching

Weeds are competition that your plants don't need. Because rhododendrons have so many surface roots, they are easily damaged by chemical sprays and hoeing. Hand weeding is fairly safe but the best idea is to use mulch, which stops many weeds becoming established and makes it far easier to remove those that do.

Mulching also helps to conserve soil moisture, lessens soil compaction and insulates the surface roots from temperature extremes.

Compost, rotted sawdust, rotted straw, used potting mix and bark chips are all suitable mulches. A mixture of fine- and medium-grade bark chips is attractive and functional. The larger pieces tend to rise to the surface and prevent the fine moisture-holding bark from blowing away.

Avoid mounding excessive mulch up against the trunk or main stems of larger rhododendrons. It may damage or soften the bark, leading to fungal or viral diseases.

Diseases

Most of the rhododendron diseases that you will occasionally encounter, such as botrytis, galls, rust and powdery mildew, are quite easily controlled with good ventilation, plant hygiene and common fungicides.

Root rot, especially the fungus *Phytophthora cinnamomi*, can be a problem, particularly in poorly drained soil. Prevention – making sure the plants are not too crowded and that the drainage is satisfactory – is the best method of control. Soil fungicides can

be used to prevent or control root rot but in most cases only one or two plants are affected and that can be tolerated.

Phytophthora syringae is a closely related fungus that causes a dieback effect on the branches. *Phomopsis* is another dieback disease, one that mainly affects azaleas. It slowly destroys twigs and branches and can prove fatal, although this usually takes several years. If odd branches show signs of wilting and yellow foliage yet there is no sign of frost damage, suspect phomopsis dieback. The disease can be controlled by removing any affected branches and spraying with an appropriate fungicide.

Pestalotia fungi cause sunburn-like markings of the foliage, particularly around the margins and tips of the leaves. Although clearly not sunburn, which usually scorches the center of the leaf, this disease can be difficult to differentiate from fertilizer burn. If no fertilizer has been used, you should suspect *Pestalotia*. Many fungicides will control this problem.

Early stages of powdery mildew on a deciduous azalea.

Severe thrip damage on a rhododendron showing the typical silvered foliage.

Azalea leaf gall is a fungal disease that attacks the new growth and the flowers. It causes an unsightly thickening and distorting of foliage and petals and can spread quickly in cool, moist weather. Picking off affected leaves and petals and spraying with a suitable fungicide will control the disease. However, this is mainly a cosmetic problem that generally causes little long-term damage.

Bud blast or bud blight is a fungal disease that attacks unopened buds, causing them to turn brown and fail to open. It would be difficult to tell apart from frost damage were it not for the fine black filaments (coremia) that develop on the bud. Infected buds should be removed and destroyed and the plant treated with a fungicide. Copper-based sprays are effective.

Ovulinia petal blight is a fungus that destroys the flowers as they open. It starts as pinhead-sized, watery, brown spots and gradually the whole flower becomes a slimy mess. This disease can spread quickly in cool, moist, spring weather. Good ventilation helps to control it but spraying with a fungicide is usually also necessary. The disease spores winter over in the soil, so the soil should be drenched with a fungicide during winter in areas where outbreaks are known to occur.

Many rhododendron leaves roll along the midrib, curl down and may develop purple spots in winter. These are not signs of a disease but appear to be related to cold weather stress.

Ring-like purple spotting on the foliage is a disease: a virus common with *R. griffithianum* hybrids such as those of the 'Loderi' grex. Although unsightly and sometimes the cause of premature leaf drop, the disease is virtually impossible to eradicate and is something you have to live with if you wish to grow these otherwise superb hybrids.

Pests

Few of the pests that attack rhododendrons are life threatening and provided you are prepared to put up with a few chewed leaves the damage is seldom serious.

Caterpillars, weevils, sawfly larvae and cutworms all cause damage by chewing the foliage and occasionally the buds and flowers. Most can be removed by hand or controlled with safe insecticides.

Azalea leaf miners can cause significant damage by destroying the foliage and retarding growth. These small caterpillars, which are common on evergreen azaleas, start life within the leaf and feed by burrowing (mining) between the upper and lower surfaces of the leaf. Later, when they become too large to remain within the leaf, they emerge and make a shelter by rolling over the tip of the leaf. Because the pest is inside the leaf, systemic insecticides are the only really effective control.

Thrips, lace bugs and spider mites may all be found on the underside of rhododendron leaves.

Leaf roller damage on an azalea leaf.

They can cause severe damage by rasping the foliage and sucking the sap. Their presence is usually indicated by leaves that develop silver-gray upper surfaces. An examination of the undersurface will reveal a sticky brown honeydew deposit, which can lead to the development of sooty mold diseases. Oil sprays and other safe insecticides can control these pests but it is very important to get complete coverage.

Damage from root-feeding weevil and beetle larvae can be a serious problem, especially with container plants. In the garden these pests are seldom present in sufficient numbers to cause great damage but in a pot they can quickly kill a plant by eating away most of the roots. An occasional sprinkle of soil insecticide will prevent such potential disasters. Rhododendron weevils will also chew the foliage. However, if the larvae are controlled, the adults are rarely a serious problem. Weevils feed at night and may be removed by hand.

Pruning

Rhododendrons don't need regular pruning; all they require is an occasional trimming to keep them neat and compact.

Dead-heading – removing of old flowers and seed heads – is often all the trimming required. Removing the seed heads allows the plant to channel its energies into growth rather than seed production and if while dead-heading you remove any crowded, weak or diseased branches close to the main stem and pinch out the tip buds from any non-flowering stems, you'll produce an evenly shaped bush with strong lateral branching and dense growth.

Sometimes you do have to go a little further. Although rhododendron trimming is not complicated, there are a few points to consider.

Any pruning is best done immediately after flowering because this allows the maximum time for regrowth and lessens the effect on the following season's flowering. Because the flower buds form in the late summer and fall, late pruning limits the amount of bud-bearing regrowth that can develop before the buds are initiated.

Start by thinning out the center of the bush to improve the air circulation. Cut back any spindly or diseased branches and remove any congested growth. Shaping the bush is now just a matter of cutting back any overly long branches and evening up the growth. Always cut back to a whorl of leaves because that is where the most vigorous buds are located.

Evergreen azaleas will usually re-shoot from anywhere on the plant and can be sheared to shape. Compact small-leafed azaleas are ideal subjects for hedging and topiary. More precise shaping is possible but it is seldom necessary to do anything more than head back any extra vigorous growth and remove damaged or weak wood.

If necessary, prune deciduous azaleas immediately after flowering. Cut the bush back to four or five main branches. You can be severe, as the new growth that develops will often be very vigorous. Pinch it back before it gets too long. This encourages lateral branching and helps to produce strong, healthy branches rather than the spindly twigs often seen on deciduous azaleas.

Very overgrown plants can be cut back to stumps but heavy pruning should be done with care because rhododendrons are sometimes reluctant to re-shoot from bare wood. Although a well-established plant will generally recover, it is often better to prune in easier stages over two seasons. Hard-pruned plants can take several years before resuming normal flowering and further shaping is almost certain to be required as the growth develops.

Feeding

Rhododendrons are not heavy feeders. Most of their needs can be met by incorporating an all-purpose acidic plant food in with their mulch. Slow-release granules are also an effective feeding method and mild liquid fertilizers can be applied during the growing season.

Any fertilizers should be watered in well because it is very easy to burn the surface roots, resulting in scorched leaves or foliage and even stem tip dieback if the burning is more severe.

Deciduous azaleas and rhododendrons play an important role in this spring garden.

While fertilizers can be used throughout the growing season, cease feeding at the end of summer or the plants may still have soft growth when the first frosts occur. Commercial growers often apply sulfate of potash in the fall to help ripen the soft growth before winter. Although this is important for commercial growers, who feed their plants well into fall to get the maximum, it is unnecessary for home gardeners provided a natural fall ripening period is allowed for.

Transplanting

Because rhododendrons have compact, shallow root systems with few heavy roots, they are very easily transplanted at almost any time of the year. Other than your ability to lift it, there is no restriction on the size of plant that can be transplanted.

The first step is to prepare the destination site. Dig a hole to what you think will be roughly the depth of the plant's roots, then increase the diameter and depth of the hole, working in compost as you dig. You'll regret not doing this first if you lift the plant and then find some unforeseen complication at the new planting site.

With the planting site prepared, you can lift the rhododendron. Dig around the plant well away from the main stem and take as large a root ball as you can manage. You should find that even a large rhododendron has most of its roots in the top 20 in (50 cm) of soil.

The next step, lifting the plant, is fraught with difficulties. Underestimating the weight of a mature rhododendron and its ball of roots is a sure way to damage your back. Sometimes the plant can be slid onto a sack or tarp and dragged to its destination or you may be able to maneuver a wheelbarrow under the shrub, but often you will need assistance to hoist the plant onto a barrow or trolley.

Before replanting, check that the hole is about the right depth – you don't want to have to lift the plant again if you can avoid it. When the plant is in the right position, backfill around it, making sure to eliminate any air pockets under the root ball. Other than the usual staking, mulching and watering, little in the way of after-care is required. Most rhododendrons carry on growing apparently unchecked and can even be moved in flower.

CHAPTER 9

Propagation

Despite the huge range of plants available from garden centers and nurseries, enthusiasts eventually want to propagate their own rhododendrons.

Raising plants from seed is the simplest propagation method, but unless you are interested only in species, the natural variation of seedlings means you will need to propagate rhododendrons vegetatively. In other words, by using parts from existing plants.

The most common vegetative method is the cutting. Small lengths of stem removed from the parent plant can be induced to develop roots if kept under controlled conditions and may then be grown as a new plant, identical to its parent.

Other common vegetative techniques include layering, aerial layering and grafting. Although the methods vary depending on the type of rhododendron being propagated, cuttings are by far the most common.

Seed

Species and new hybrids must be raised from seed, but with the exception of some of the deciduous azalea strains, seed is rarely a practical method for propagating cultivars and selected varieties as they do not reproduce true to type.

Growing rhododendrons from seed is not difficult, but depending on the type, it can take 18 months to five years before the first flowers open. Tree-sized rhododendrons may not flower until they are over eight years old.

Seed may be bought, produced by hybridizing or collected from plants that have been naturally pollinated.

Seed houses specializing in shrubs and trees usually stock a wide range of rhododendron species and many rhododendron societies supply seed to their members. When you buy rhododendron species seed you will find that some types are numbered. These collectors' numbers refer to the original specimen collected in the wild. They are a useful way of identifying local variations in a species but are not of great significance for the beginner.

Determining exactly when the seed is ready to harvest is not always easy. The seed must be ripe, but leave it too late and the pods will burst and scatter the seed. Often there will be color changes or drying as the seed pods near maturity but occasionally you may have to harvest slightly unripe pods and ripen them indoors to avoid losing the seed. Tying a small paper bag over the ripening pods to catch falling seed is sometimes possible.

Sow your seed on a finely sieved 50/50 mixture of sphagnum moss and peat- or bark-based potting mix. Do not cover the seed, just sow it on the surface and gently moisten it with a fine mist. Kept lightly shaded and moist, it germinates in 10 days to six weeks depending on the type.

While dry seed keeps reasonably well, it germinates best if sown immediately after harvest, which is usually in the fall. However, unless you can keep the young seedlings protected, it is best to delay sowing until spring because fall-germinated seedlings are rather tender and may collapse over winter.

Rhododendron seeds are very fine and the young seedlings are tiny and slow growing. They are generally not suitable for sowing outdoors either in trays or the open ground and will do far better if grown under controlled conditions. Aim for high humidity, steady, even warmth (around 64°F/18°C) and give them an occasional diluted liquid feeding.

Although most seedling plants are potted once they have their first true leaves, rhododendrons are

Rhododendron 'Golden Wit'

frequently too small to handle conveniently at this stage. No harm will come to them if they are left to develop in the seed tray provided their nutrient requirements are met. Rhododendron seedlings normally transplant well and establish quickly.

Cuttings

Most rhododendrons can be grown from cuttings, the methods varying slightly with the different styles of growth. It is vital that the cutting environment is humid because any wilting will stress the cuttings, possibly fatally.

A propagating frame with a built-in mister and bottom heat is highly recommended, though enclosing the cutting trays or pots in plastic tents works reasonably well.

Softwood cuttings are taken from the new growth before it has become firm and often before it

is fully expanded. Softwood cuttings strike and develop quickly because they are taken from the most actively growing part of the plant. They are, however, easily damaged and prone to wilting under the slightest moisture stress.

Commercial growers with sophisticated propagating equipment generally prefer softwood cuttings, but home gardeners, who usually operate under more primitive conditions, have more success with semi-ripe cuttings.

A semi-ripe cutting is simply a softwood cutting that has matured slightly. Its foliage (apart from the extreme tip) will usually be fully expanded and the stem will be firm yet pliable. Semi-ripe cuttings are usually available from late spring until mid-fall.

Tip cuttings strike best. The size of the cutting varies with the plant being propagated and the stage of growth. Softwood cuttings are seldom more than 4 in (10 cm) long, while semi-ripe cuttings tend to be larger, typically around 6 in (15 cm), because the internodal length (the stem length between the leaves) increases as the growth matures and expands.

Very small softwood cuttings, such as those of evergreen azaleas, can simply be snapped off at the base. Larger softwood and semi-ripe cuttings are removed with pruning shears and usually strike best if cut at a node.

Carefully strip the leaves from the lower nodes. Although soft cuttings are easily damaged, most leaves come away cleanly if they are removed with a quick upward action after being pulled downwards just enough to break the joint between the leaf and the stem.

If the leaves of the cutting are very large, it may be necessary to trim the foliage to cut down the moisture lost through transpiration and to enable more cuttings to fit in the container or tray. The foliage can be cut back by about half.

Before inserting a cutting into the propagating mixture, dip it in rooting hormone. This is available in liquid, gel or powder form and can be varied in

Cuttings before and after preparation. Left: rhododendron; center: deciduous azalea; right: evergreen azalea.

Rhododendron 'Countess of Haddington', with mildly fragrant flowers.

strength to suit the type of cutting. I find that the semi-ripe strength is suitable for most cuttings.

I prefer a propagating medium made from a finely sieved 50/50 mixture of perlite and bark-based potting mix, but any well-aerated soilless mix is capable of producing good results. Very soft cuttings may need to be dibbled into place to avoid bruising, but most cuttings will not be damaged if they are gently pushed into place. The cuttings can be spaced so that they are just touching, but if they are going under mist they should not overlap because leaves that are covered by others will not receive any mist.

Wounding

Some rhododendrons are slow to strike roots. Wounding – removing a small strip of bark – by making a shallow downward cut along the side of the cutting immediately above the base, exposes a greater area of cambium (the layer of cells below the bark from which new growth occurs) which can speed up the rooting process and may also produce a better root structure. It is generally restricted to shrubby large-leafed rhododendrons and is seldom used with alpines, small-leafed rhododendrons or azaleas.

Cutting methods for various types of rhododendron

Evergreen azaleas and small-leafed alpine rhododendrons

Softwood cuttings may be taken as soon as the new spring growth is firm enough to handle. These may be very small. Cuttings can be taken right through until early fall but after early summer they will be less vigorous than those taken in spring and will not be as well-established by winter. The early cuttings will strike in about six to eight weeks under mist, or up to 12 weeks or more without mist.

Broad-leafed rhododendrons

Take semi-ripe cuttings from early summer through to mid-fall. Unless you have a misting system, it may be difficult to stop early cuttings from wilting. Those taken after mid-summer may have flower buds but remove them as they are an unwanted drain on the cuttings' limited resources.

Early cuttings may strike before winter but later ones will probably not get under way before the following spring. Mist and bottom heat will greatly accelerate root formation and increase the strike rate.

Deciduous azaleas

Some deciduous azaleas, such as true Mollis hybrids, are difficult to grow from cuttings. Others, particularly the R. *occidentale* hybrids, strike easily from soft to semi-ripe cuttings taken in mid- to late spring.

Deciduous azalea cuttings must strike well before winter otherwise they will probably collapse before spring. It is often best to shelter the first-year cuttings. If this is not possible, layering or aerial layering may be better methods to use.

Opposite: Deciduous azalea '*Giant Orange*', an Ilam hybrid.

Layering

Layering is a good way to propagate rhododendrons that are difficult to strike from cuttings, but it is slow and may take up to two years to produce results.

Low-growing rhododendrons, particularly evergreen azaleas, often self-layer where their stems touch the ground. These natural layers may be removed and potted or replanted elsewhere.

You can simulate this natural layering by keeping a stem in contact with the soil. With time, roots will form. Start by selecting a pliable stem that can be bent to ground level. Scrape out a shallow trench where the branch touches the ground. Make a shallow cut on the lower side of the stem, dust the wound with a little rooting hormone powder, then with wire hoops peg down the stem in the trench. Stake the growing tip with a bamboo cane to make it upright, then refill the trench, mounding the soil up slightly so that it doesn't sink.

Rhododendron 'Fastuosum Flore Pleno', one of the few semi-double true rhododendrons.

Aerial layering

You often find that a rhododendron has no new stems near ground level. Such bushes may be propagated by aerial layering, which effectively takes the soil to the stem.

Start by selecting a length of firm stem that still has green bark. Older wood will strike but it takes longer. Aerial layering can be done any time such material is available. Remove the foliage from around the immediate area and make a shallow upward cut into the stem. Lift the flap of bark and wedge it open with a matchstick. Lightly dust the wound with rooting hormone powder and wrap the stem with wet sphagnum moss. Then wrap the ball of sphagnum in black polyethylene and secure it with wire ties or tape. The moss will keep the wound from drying out and healing over, and roots will eventually form at the wound. The layer will take about 10-12 months to strike well. It can be left through winter, because if the plant can survive freezing, the layer should also. However, this method has not been well-documented, so it is a case of trial and error. When it is apparent that a good root system has formed, the layer, complete with the sphagnum, may be removed and potted.

Rhododendron 'Frank Baum'

Grafting

If you have a large garden, there are few plants more spectacular than the fragrant, pink-flowered *Rhododendron griffithianum* hybrids. However, these plants, and a few others, can be difficult to obtain because they do not always grow well on their own roots and often require grafting.

Obviously for grafting you need a rootstock. 'Cunningham's White' is one of the most widely used and is preferable to *R. ponticum*, an earlier favorite, because it doesn't produce as many suckers (unwanted growths from the rootstock) as *R. ponticum*. It is easily propagated by cuttings or layers. Alternatively, you may find a nursery that sells small plants suitable for use as grafting stocks.

The best time to graft is when growth begins in early spring, but before the new foliage expands. Grafting requires that the cambium of the stock and scion (the variety to be grafted onto the stock) is kept in contact long enough to fuse and this involves some trimming and fitting to get a good match. The saddle graft and the side wedge are commonly used techniques.

Practice making the cuts with a few old twigs before sacrificing any valuable plants. Bind the stock and scion together with grafting tape if you have it, otherwise plumber's thread tape or adhesive tape will do. This is awkward at first but you'll soon get the idea.

To keep the freshly grafted plants growing and to prevent drying out, keep them in a warm, humid environment. Fill a shallow tray with gravel, then pour in water until it's just level with the surface of the gravel. Sit the pots on the gravel and the water will ensure that the atmosphere remains humid. If the tray can be covered with a plastic tent, so much the better. Grafts in the garden should be covered with a plastic bag, making sure that the bag cannot dislodge the graft if it moves in the wind.

Once the scion is growing well and the graft has callused over, the tape can be slit or removed. Don't leave this too long or you may find the tape starts to cut into the stem.

Sources

Aesthetic Gardens
PO Box 1362
Boring, OR 97009
Fax (503) 663-6672
Website: www.agardens.com
Extensive selection of rare and unusual rhododendron hybrids and species, and evergreen and deciduous azaleas. Ships to Canada.

American Rhododendron Society
11 Pinecrest Drive
Fortuna, CA 95540
Tel (707)-725-3043
Fax (707)-725-1217
Website: www.rhododendron.org
Chapters throughout the United States, Canada and internationally. Contact for referral to local branch. Six levels of membership starting at $28.00 annual dues. Chapters publish plant recommendations for local climate.

Asandy Rhododendron
41610 SE Coalman Road
Sandy, OR 97055
Tel (503) 668-4830; Fax (503) 275-9271
Website: www.rhodo.com
Rare and unusual rhododendron hybrids and species. Ships to Canada.

Azalea Society of America
PO Box 34536
West Bethesda, MD 20827-0536
Tel (301) 365-0692
Website: www.azaleas.org
Publishes quarterly, The Azalean.

Azalea Trace
5510 Stephen Reid Road
Huntingtown, MD 20639
Tel (301) 855-2305 or (410) 257-0837
Over 500 varieties, container-grown.

The Bovees Nursery
1737 SW Coronado Street
Portland, OR 97219
Toll-Free Tel 1-800-435-9250
Tel (503) 244-9341
Website: www.bovees.com
Over 400 hybrids and species vireya rhododendrons. Ships to Canada.

Carlson's Gardens
PO Box 305
South Salem, NY 10590
Tel (914) 763-5958
Fax (707) 202-2560
Website: www.carlsonsgardens.com
Specializes in hardy rhododendrons and azaleas. No shipping to CA or Canada.

Fraser's Thimble Farms
175 Arbutus Road
Salt Spring Island, BC V6K 1A3
Tel/Fax (250) 537-5788
Website: www.thimblefarms.com
Email: thimble@saltspring.com
Rare-plant specialists. Order by mail, fax or email; no phone orders. Ships to U.S.

Girard Nurseries
PO Box 428
Geneva, OH 44041
Tel (216) 466-2881
Website: www.girardnurseries.com
Rhododendrons, deciduous and evergreen azaleas.

Granite Hill Gardens
PO Box 609
Manchester ME 04351-0609
Toll-Free Tel 1-888-267-0868
Tel (207) 623-3799
Fax (703) 940-7405
Website: www.granitehillgardens.com
Cold-hardy Maine-tested rhododendrons and azaleas. Ships to Canada.

Greer Gardens
1280 Goodpasture Island Road
Eugene, OR 97401
Toll-Free Tel 1-800-548-0111
Tel (503) 686-8266
Fax (503) 686-0910
Website: www.greergardens.com
Extensive selection of rhododendrons, azaleas, trees and shrubs, vines, and bonsai stock. Ships to Canada.

Homeplace Garden Nursery
PO Box 300, Harden Bridge Road
Commerce, GA 30529
Tel (706) 335-2892
Primarily rhododendrons plus azaleas and companion plants.

Lazy K Nursery, Inc.
705 Wright Road
Pine Mountain, GA 31822
Tel (706) 663-4991
Website: www.lazyknursery.com
Specialists in native azaleas and deciduous rhododendrons, all winter-hardy to Zone 6.

Nuccio's Nurseries
3555 Chaney Trail
Altadena, CA 91001
Tel (626) 794-3383
Specialists in azaleas.

The Plant Farm
177 Vesuvius Bay Road
Salt Spring Island, BC V8K 1K3
Tel (250) 537-5995
Good selection of flowering trees and shrubs, including hardy Finnish rhododendrons.

Pushepetappa Gardens
2317 Washington Street
Franklinton, LA 70438
Tel (504)) 839-5311 or 839-4930
Rhododendrons and native azalea hybrids for the south.

Rare Find Nursery
957 Patterson Road GSG
Jackson, NJ 08527
Tel (732) 833-0613
Newest, most unusual hardy azaleas and rhododendrons.

Rhododendron Species Foundation
PO Box 3798
Federal Way, WA 98063
Tel (253) 838-4646; Fax (253) 838-4686
Website: www.halcyon.com/rsf/
Sells plants and oversees Western North American Rhododendron Species Project.

Roslyn Nursery
211 Burrs Lane
Dix Hills NY 11746
Tel (516) 643 9347; Fax (516) 427 0894
Website: www.roslynnursery.com
Rare and exotic varieties of rhododendrons and azaleas, including many specialist hybrids. Ships to Canada.

Shepherd Hill Farm, Inc.
200 Peekskill Hollow Road
Putnam Valley, NY 10579
Tel (914) 528-5917; Fax (914) 528-8343
Website: www.shepherdhillfarm.com
Specializes in East Coast-hardy varieties, large-leaf and small-leafed. Large selection of Dexter hybrids. No shipping to AZ, CA, OR, WA or Canada.

Singing Tree Gardens
1975 Blake Road
PO Box 2684
McKinleyville, CA 95519
Tel (707) 839-8777
Website: www.singtree.com
Specialists in fragrant rhododendrons

Sonoma Horticultural Nursery
3970 Azalea Ave
Sebastopol, CA 95472
Tel (707) 823-6832.
Rhododendrons, azaleas and companion plants.

Woodland Nurseries
2151 Camilla Road
Mississauga, ON L5A 2K1
Tel (905) 277-2961; Fax (905) 277-0650
Website: www.echo-on.net/~woodland
Elepidote and lepidote rhododendrons, deciduous and semi-evergreen azaleas. All cold-hardy.

Index